"Anyone who has lost a child will fir
story. She is a beacon of light that he
by guiding them home through scripture, analogies, and her real story of heartbreak. You will experience a range of emotions as she makes you feel a little less alone in your waves of grief. This is a must read for those who have experienced an unimaginable loss. What is it really like? How will I survive? Candice will walk you through it step by step, page by page."

—Mikella Van Dyke
Owner and Author of *Chasing Sacred*

"I cried for every page in the first half, or maybe two thirds, of the book – not only because Candice brings the reader into the depths of her own suffering, but also because of the profound strength she finds in God and in herself. Whatever loss you have experienced or may experience in the future, this book provides hope that what feels impossible is possible – moving forward, living, loving and remembering. *Hope (Amidst the Stories I Told Myself): How to Find Hope in Love and Loss* encourages us that no matter how short a life or how big a loss it is possible to find and share strength, joy and hope."

—Megan Harley
Educator and Leadership Coach Nonprofit Manager

"Candice truly captured the emotions mixed with the comfort of faith and prayer during a time of infant loss. *Hope (Amidst the Stories I Told Myself)*, is straight to the heart, allowing the reader to see her vulnerabilities by admitting her strengths and weaknesses, and how faith and laughter helped her family to grow stronger through grief. As a therapist I hear many stories of grief and loss but reading it here put power in the words in a way that I try to get many clients to come to terms with in order to heal and grow, as the DeLeeuw's have done. Wonderfully Written book of hope and healing."

—Jessie Napoli
LCMHC-A, Play and EMDR Therapist

"It's so much easier to run away from your own suffering than it is to find God's purpose in it and live it out. Candice has been doing the opposite for years. She has shared her story openly to bring quiet hope and strength at just the right moment to other struggling pilgrims. This book takes us deep into the journey of the heart when life's circumstances threaten to shatter us. We find as we read her story, we connect with our own disappointments and find her example of strength gives us courage to carry on. Thank you, dear Candice for writing this beautiful book!"

—Tonia Lyon
Unscripted Life Personal and Professional Development Coach

"Profoundly healing. DeLeeuw pens her heart onto paper in a way that can only be possible with the awesome grace of God. Poignant and raw and infused with hope, her meaningful message will captivate the depths of your soul while making it hard for you to put down her truthful words. Any tears that ensue may miraculously wash away your own pain and grief as you and the author heal together, one word and one chapter at a time. Beautifully, tragically real."

—Kristi Cruise
CEO of Living Libraries, Author of *The LiLi Key*

HOPE

(Admidst the Stories I Told Myself)

How to Find Hope in Love and Loss

Foreword by Andrew J. Lodge, MD

CANDICE DELEEUW

DEDICATED IN LOVING MEMORY OF
ALEXANDER COLE DELEEUW

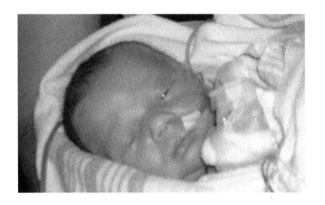

*The mention of my child's name may bring tears to my eyes, but it never
fails to bring music to my ears. If you are really my friend, let me hear
the music of her name. It soothes my broken heart and sings to my soul!*
~Author unknown ~

CONTENTS

FOREWORD

By Andrew J. Lodge, MD

No one should have to endure the death of their baby. Unfortunately, in the specialty of congenital heart surgery (operating on infants, children and adults with birth defects of the heart), this is an event that I have witnessed on too many occasions. Open heart surgery has only been practiced successfully since the 1950's. Over the course of that time, the mortality rate has dramatically decreased. Currently for congenital heart surgery as a whole, survival after surgery approaches 98%. That doesn't matter at all however, if your child happens to be in the 2% that doesn't survive.

Having practiced for seventeen years in this specialty, I have had the unfortunate opportunity to observe a substantial number of parents suffer through the loss of a child, including newborn babies. I'm sure there is nothing that can adequately prepare a human being to cope with such a tragedy. As such, I have observed a very wide range of reactions, responses, emotions, and behaviors from parents. In fact, depending on the circumstances, I have experienced this same range of all of the above myself. This has as much to do with me becoming a parent myself during the course of my career as it does with the individual nature of each case and my relationship with the patient and family

The author of this book and her family are special to me

for a number of reasons. When I first met the DeLeeuw family, they were new parents of their first born child. Alex was born with hypoplastic left heart syndrome, a condition in which the left side of the heart is so underdeveloped that it cannot support the circulation. While this condition was generally fatal until the 1980's, a series of complex surgical procedures now exist to treat it. These operations do not cure the heart defect, but they allow the child to survive and grow with a permanently abnormal circulation based on the presence of only a single functional pumping chamber (ventricle). Taking care of these children involves a lifelong partnership between the family, patient, and physicians. The first of the series of operations, the Norwood procedure, is in the highest risk category of operations that we do, with a hospital survival of only about 85%. This, an unimaginably stressful situation for most of us, was what the DeLeeuw's were facing when I met them. Despite this, their young ages, and their relative unfamiliarity with the medical system, they projected a certain degree of calm, grace, and even humor. I will always remember this about them.

When we performed Alex's first operation at only six days old, the procedure seemed to go well. Despite that, after surgery we experienced a number of complications that ultimately did not allow Alex to recover and left the family having to consider the options. These options were not good ones and essentially consisted of continuing to support the baby which involved subjecting him to further pain and discomfort, or withdrawing support and allowing him to pass away as comfortably as possible. I cannot fathom how it would feel to be faced with such a decision about my own child, let alone my first-born.

In this book, Candice DeLeeuw shares her experience in anticipation it can provide some support and a glimmer of hope for life which comes after such a tragedy. In her own words, if she helps even one person in a similar situation, it will be worth all the effort. This is an incredibly courageous effort. Besides just the time and commitment required to write this book, I am sure it was not an easy journey for Candice to relive her experience. With the expansion of the internet and the resources it provides, there are a number of means of support for families experiencing difficult times with the terminal illness of a child or other loved one. If you are reading this book, it is likely you are facing such a situation. I thank Candice for answering the calling she heard to write this book and I sincerely hope you can use it to help you in your journey, and it helps you to find peace and comfort in the end.

— Andrew J. Lodge, MD
Associate Professor of Surgery and Pediatrics
Division of Cardiovascular and Thoracic Surgery
Duke University Health System

PREFACE

I f you have lost a child, spouse, friend, or parent, this book is for you. I wrote this book because, after losing our son, I read at least twenty-five books in six months on child loss. None of them told me what I needed to know, which was, although what happened was not okay, I would be okay. I wanted to know the survivors' details. Too many of the books glossed over these details and were instead filled with statistics and "doctor" talk. If you are looking for details—reminders that you're not alone in this journey—this is it.

If you have ever struggled with the "stories you tell yourself," this book is for you, too. Although losing a child may not resonate with everyone, I'm confident that most people can relate to the many other losses: friendship, job, a clean bill of health, marriage, or a dream. We all can get lost in the voices in our head. Join me as we navigate these stories together.

Hope is always on the horizon.

CHAPTER ONE

TAKING A CRUISE
(I CAN PLAN EVERYTHING)

I have always dreamed of going on a cruise, but every time I look at them online it feels overwhelming. How do you pack for all those days for all these people in such a small tiny cabin which looks the size of my bathroom? Yes, I know I can ask friends who have been. I can hire a travel agent to do it all for me. If I am completely honest that is not my personality. You see I am a planner. I am not exaggerating. I do not have one calendar but three: one whiteboard monthly calendar (color coded of course) for the whole family to see, the calendar in my phone shared with my husband so we can both keep up with all the shenanigans, and then the golden nugget... my desk calendar which has space for me to plan out all my "to do's" where I can add those cute planner stickers. Excessive? Possibly.

Maybe you still aren't grasping my intense desires to plan. You know those people who take their family to Walt Disney's Magic Kingdom and just walk around enjoying everything at a leisurely pace? Oh yeah, that is not me. I have researched when all the shows, parades, parade routes, and reserved my Fast Pass tickets. I have color coded, grouped in "lands" and popularity, the order we will ride the rides. I know where we will eat lunch and dinner based on how long it will take to get around. I have it nailed down to a science. Did I mention I also laminate this list? My father-in-law, an Orlando resident and Disney passholder, said he had never seen so much of Disney in one day. Mission Accomplished.

So, you can say I have planning problems. One hiccup to my planning problems is God. His plans and my plans don't always go hand in hand. Take my husband for instance. The year was 2004, I was home for the summer and beginning my student teaching experience in the fall. This was my last summer where I was not going to have to be an "adult." I just wanted a "summer fling." A no strings attached, let's just have fun kind of guy. Insert my husband, fresh from a long-term relationship and the Air Force. He was the "bad boy" from our graduating class. Let's just cue the music for "Summer Lovin" from Grease to get you in the right mind set. This "bad boy" and "good girl" quickly went from dating in June to engaged five months later, and then married by February. We packed up and moved across the country from Michigan to North Carolina to follow a job opportunity a week later. We were on the fast track, but realized we needed to get to know each other before we had any children. We did what sensible adults do, we bought a dog and would wait five years to have children. The following weekend after purchasing the extremely adorable Shiatzu, just three months after we wed, we discovered we were pregnant! We were still in the "pee with the door closed" phase of our marriage so you can only imagine the shock as my husband is standing outside of the bathroom door with the pregnancy test box and I am on the other side with the stick reading two very bright lines. He is telling me two lines means pregnant and I am confident one of those lines *will* disappear, that *has* to be how this test works. God must be laughing from the heavens as He watches my plans crumble and His unfold.

No, I have not yet been on a cruise. I had to plan for my first child, which felt like planning a cruise. There are so many details. Which doctor do I choose? At which hospital do I deliver? How will I decorate the nursery? What name will we pick? How will I keep this little person *alive*?

Everything about my pregnancy was normal, except it wasn't. Deep inside I knew *something* was wrong. I chalked it up to first time mom nerves. In September 2005, an insurance company came to the middle school where I was teaching. The agents met with each staff member individually to answer questions and discuss the importance of keeping insurance policies current. Being a new mom, in a new state, and with my first job I had questions. The health plan had an add on for ICU coverage. For just $11 a month it covered you or your unborn child's ICU bed space and then you would have 30 days to add the child to the ICU coverage if needed. After prodding from the sales rep, they saw "sucker" across my forehead, I thought, *"I'll add it, why not?"*

We are still in newlywed bliss a few weeks later when my husband was sent to Ohio for job training for four weeks. A few weeks into the training we decided to meet halfway for the weekend in Berkley, West Virginia. We asked the hotel receptionist where we could find a good place to walk Gizmo our dog (you know the one we got so we wouldn't get pregnant). The receptionist told us about the beautiful cemetery next door where many people walk. Instead of going to the main entrance we cut across where our hotel was located. For hundreds of feet we walked in silence as we noticed the gravestone markers around us. The area we cut through was designated for children. My stomach churned. When we got to the pathway, I looked at my husband and said, "I can never bury my child. I can't imagine how hard it would be to lose your baby." My husband just held me in his arms as we stood in silence for all the lives lost and the parents left behind in mourning. We had no idea how big of a statement this would be for us.

The night before my induction, January 25, my husband and my mom were putting together the pack-n-play in the living room of our first home. I sat down in the recliner as gracefully as any nine-month pregnant woman and sighed. I said out loud what I had been holding in for quite some time. I spoke the words which had been haunting me, the feelings I just couldn't shake, "I feel like I am having a baby tomorrow, but I don't feel like we are bringing him home."

They both stopped what they were doing and stared at me. Why would I say something such as this? What would make me think this?

The answer is planning. Amidst all my planning, of the nursery, the name, the clothes, the bottle type, and everything in between, I never really felt like it was for our son. God was planning something. Something far bigger than I could have ever imagined. The extra insurance…. God's planning. The realization parents sometimes have to bury their babies… God's planning. All along He was beginning to prepare my heart because if I been told these plans in advance, I would have run from them.

It's funny how we want God to answer all our prayers and to show us everything. So often we don't even want to take a step unless we know the outcome will be good. Never do we throw ourselves into a situation we know will hurt us in the end. Never do we ask for such pain, sorrow, shame, or guilt to penetrate our souls. Frequently, we ask God for the next step, but we are only willing to take it if it is wrapped in a pretty package sealed with hope and promises of greatness.

Just as most 18-year old's do, I began contemplating my

purpose in this life. I wanted to know that my life mattered and I was doing what God has placed in me to do. It was in 2001 when I read The Prayer of Jabez — Breakthrough to the Blessed Life by Bruce Wilkinson and was inspired.[1] I was a Young Life (YL) leader and I wanted more ministry, more conversations, more of His inner workings into my life.

I began to pray the Prayer of Jabez from:

9 Jabez was more honorable than his brothers. His mother had named him Jabez, saying, "I gave birth to him in pain."
10 Jabez cried out to the God of Israel, "Oh, that you would bless me and enlarge my territory! Let your hand be with me, and keep me from harm so that I will be free from pain."
And God granted his request.
1 Chronicles 4:9–10.

Asking God to enlarge *my* territory. I prayed this prayer for three solid years. Seeing glimpses of these Jabez appointments spoken about in this book and excitement in how God was using me. During my college years, the book became a tool, a relevant in my hands tool to ask God for more in order to glorify Him. Little did I know, my biggest Jabez appointment was headed my way. These years were just the beginning of what God was going to do through my life. I didn't know these were just the preparations for it and it would make an impact on me for decades.

Just as Jonah in the Old Testament, if I knew what I was up against I would have ran.

1 The word of the Lord came to Jonah son of Amittai: 2 "Go to the great city of Nineveh and preach against it, because its wickedness has come up before me."

3 But Jonah ran away from the Lord and headed for Tarshish.
He went down to Joppa, where he found a ship bound for
that port. After paying the fare, he went aboard and sailed
for Tarshish to flee from the Lord.
Jonah 1:1–3

God's plans were not revealed to me; therefore I did not run.

> Has there ever been something in your life
> you too would have ran from if you
> knew how it would turn out?

As most induction mornings go, it was early to arrive, and neither of us were talkative. It was only a five-minute drive from our first home's driveway to the nearby hospital, but I remember the eerie silence in the darkness. The silence of nerves and fears. I was nervous about having a baby and all which surrounds the unknown. My heart knew it was more than just fear of labor. Pulling into the parking spot was too much, my nerves were about to explode. I couldn't even control it anymore. *Something* was wrong. Every part of me knew, there was something much bigger happening. As we opened our doors to exit the car I cried out "WAIT!" My husband looks at me and I said, "We need to pray first." Remember I was Sandy Olsson married to my Danny Zuko (from Grease) and praying together was not something we did. In this moment I did not care what he thought, I was panicking, and I was losing it. I knew I could not leave the car. Fear was paralyzing me. So, in a parked car with my husband's questioning look, I began to pray aloud. However, I really didn't know what to pray and I quickly realized I couldn't *just* pray. No, my soul was weeping. I began weeping and praying repeatedly, "God whatever is about to happen, just prepare our hearts for it." After a few minutes, a peace filled my heart. I didn't know what was going to happen, but I did know God was protecting me. I was able to wipe my tears and head into the hospital hand in hand with my shocked husband who watched me transform from an out of control blubbering mess to completely calm.

The rest of our day was fairly uneventful. Pitocin was started and my water broke around eleven AM on the way to the bathroom. I cried out, "I swear I did not just pee!" These are the things you say when you have been married less than a year and are still worried about embarrassing yourself. We watched Oprah, read magazines, and I tried to forget the episode in the car that morning. It was so uneventful when my husband left to get lunch, he returned with his haircut too.

With no progression by the evening, I was wheeled in for a c-section and delivered my perfect son. I asked the doctor two things while lying on the table doped up, "Is the baby a boy? Is he ok?" The baby was indeed a boy and he was more than ok, he scored a 9.9 on the APGAR test. When I awoke in the recovery room, I tried to get my toes to move so I could see my baby, while the nurse told me that my son was the most beautiful baby she had ever seen. Cue the music to this mother's ears. Of course, I thought she was just being nice, but she reassured me she had seen many babies and could attest that he was. The nurse was right. When I laid eyes on my perfect "little man" he was a beautiful baby. Alexander Cole DeLeeuw, was 7 pounds 10.5 ounces of perfection. He instantly captured my heart and I began to think all the worrying was over nothing.

Funny how in hindsight we can identify changes we would make if given the opportunity for a re-do. If I could go back to

January 27 there is so much I would have changed. I would have not pushed the morphine drip all night out of the fear of any pain resulting in my extreme nausea. I would not have sent my husband home to sleep and shower in the early morning. When my son was handed to me with a bottle but could not eat more than a few sucks without falling asleep, I would have pushed the issue with a nurse instead of being shrugged off. I would have asked the staff to help me reach my breakfast which was placed just out of my reach. I would have listened to my gut which was telling me something just wasn't right. When no nurse answered my call when I pushed the help button resulting in my physical sickness on my bed, somehow avoiding Alex lying in my arms; I would have asked for help instead of allowing the staff to be angry with me. I would have sucked up the pain and adjusted Alex from being cradled in my arms to lying on my chest enabling me to smell his sweet smell.

In the last hour before my mom arrived, Alex was still peacefully sleeping in my arms. I laid my right hand across his chest so I could feel him if he stopped breathing. I was fatigued. My eyes were so heavy. Over the course of the next hour I was struggling to stay awake. I watched the wall clock in front of me. Every ten minutes I checked Alex to see if he was breathing and then told myself, *"You must stay awake, you must stay awake."* This would be the last time I held him alone, without wires.

When my mother arrived at 10:00 AM, I handed my sweet boy to her to see if she could get him to eat. This continued for hours, a few sucks and then he'd fall asleep. Not once did he cry. We spent the morning taking pictures of him and loving on the most peaceful newborn. Chaos continued with my monitors beeping, rude nurses, and doctors' orders not being followed; but as far as our new parent bubble, we were in bliss.

Late afternoon, a nurse came to take Alex to the nursery to have his vitals checked. These had not been updated since he had been placed in my arms early that morning. He had still not eaten more than a few sucks here and there. Before they whisked him away, I begged for one "family picture," even though it clearly annoyed the nurse. Alex was awake and staring out the window, his eyes were wide open and his face serious. He looked like a wise old man in contemplation, as if he knew what was about to unfold.

One thing that scares me about the idea of going on a cruise is the fear of the "what-if's." The what-if the whole ship gets a stomach virus, pirates seize the ship, there is a hurricane, or a completely out of the blue Bomb Cyclone? Or what if we hit an iceberg and I somehow don't make it on the tiny boats tied to the side, but I do end up floating on a board holding the love of my life's hand… all the what-if's in the world could not have prepared us for the bubble burst that was coming.

My mother and husband were playing cards and I was resting when the "snappy" nurse we had been dealing with all day burst the bubble. She charged into our room, frantic, and angry. Loudly she said, "Let me guess. Dad, Grandma, and Mom." As she stood at the end of my bed, she said directly to me, "What color was your son when he left this room?"

I was in utter shock.

My Mom asked, "Was he yellow?"

I hesitantly said, "White."

She exclaimed, "No! He was gray! Why is your son gray? Why didn't you notice he was gray?"

I instantly felt sick and fired back, "What do you mean? What is wrong with him?"

She cut me off, "We don't know! That is why I want to

know what happened. Why didn't you notice he was gray? All the lights should be on in the room!"

I was now in defensive Momma Bear mode and yelled back, "You brought him to me at 8:00 in the morning with no one else here and handed him to me. You don't know me. You assumed I knew what to do. I had a c-section the night before and am on morphine. When the drip ran out and began to beep for over thirty minutes, you did not care. You even yelled at my mother when she asked you to take care of it. I also still have the catheter in my doctor told me this morning was to be removed. I could hardly even keep my eyes open until my mom arrived..."

She again cut me off, "What! You should have not been sleeping with your baby!"

"I KNOW, but what was I *supposed* to do. His bed was out of my reach and I can hardly reposition myself let alone get him safely into his bed!"

"You should have called a nurse!"

"Anytime a nurse came in they were angry. I didn't want to come across needy and make anyone mad. Besides what if he would have started crying? Who would have helped me then?"

"You should have called the nursery. We would have come to get him."

"How? Where is the number?"

"It is right..." she turned to point to where it is posted in my room but finds it is not there. "Well, you should have told the nurses station."

She started to storm off when I cried out, "But what is wrong with him? Will he be ok?"
She turned and coldly responded, "We don't know" and closed my door.

The cruise ship has been struck by an iceberg.

We were all stunned, paralyzed, and silent. Did this actually happen? Are we sure it is even our baby she is talking about? "Brandon, go check on Alex!" I cry out.

As my husband jumped up to rush out, the door opened, and a new nurse came in. She had heard the whole thing and had requested help. She was clearly concerned about the yelling match that just conspired in this room. Just as she walked out, Alex's pediatrician and the snappy nurse walked in. I couldn't even look at this nurse. I wanted to know about my baby, but I didn't want this nurse anywhere near him. The pediatrician informed us they didn't have the technology to determine what is wrong with our son, but they have called Duke Medical Center and they are on their way. Duke believes it is something to do with his heart. Duke told them to give him prostaglandin, to keep him stable by allowing his heart to operate like it is in the womb (keeping the ductus arteriosus open so blood can get to the rest of the body) until they can run further tests. She informed us we couldn't see him, and they will send in the Duke team to speak to us before he is airlifted.

The ship is sinking and I must be in the ice water because I am numb.

So numb was I to the details of who'd go to the hospital, who'd call my colleagues, and how I'd possibly stay back another night, that everything was a blur. I was physically and emotionally exhausted. As my friends and colleagues stepped into the hallway to prepare for the evening, several were taking shifts to stay with me, so I wasn't alone. Most importantly, they stood together and they prayed.

As they prayed the Duke Life Flight team wheeled Alexander down in an incubator so we could see him one last time. Lisa, one of the team members, had reassured us as they were preparing him for the flight in the nursery, we had the very best from Duke tonight, Edd Shope, the Neonatal Transport Coordinator. Alexander looked so tiny in this big contraption with all these scary wires and tubes keeping him alive. They allowed us to reach in and touch him one last time. In spite of how incredibly scary and confusing all of this was, I remember the eyes of Edd. When I looked at him as he spoke, there was something in his eyes which reassured me. Something in his eyes conveyed confidence, care, and trust; it filled me with peace. They wheeled him away and Edd looked back and said, "We will take care of him."

There we were left alone as our only child was taking his first flight.

You Are My Sunshine
Jimmie Davis[2]

The other night, dear, as I lay sleeping
I dreamed I held you in my arms
But when I awoke, dear, I was mistaken
And I hung my head and I cried

CHAPTER TWO

THE HURRICANE
(I CAUSED THIS)

There is something about hurricanes which makes them equally thrilling and terrifying. Living in the south, to be close to hurricanes but far enough away to not have to deal with their destructive power, is probably what makes them so interesting to me. The weather can be perfectly fine one minute, the next, a hurricane can suddenly form off the coast, with every news channel covering it. You can't help but be glued to the weather forecasts. You watch as people scramble to prepare. Some will stay and others will clog the highways, racing to get out of harm's way.

The following morning, after a drug induced sleep, I awoke hopeful and delusional. I honestly believed Duke Medical would fix what was wrong and my son and he would be back in my arms the same day. Brandon would bring him to me. Even when Brandon called with the news that it was his heart I had no idea of the severity of it all.

My husband, who had checked my mom into the hotel and went straight to the pediatric ICU at Duke Medical Center, found out the devastating news alone in the wee hours of the night. Our perfect son was born with one of the most severe heart defects, Hypoplastic Left Heart Syndrome (HLHS). Without surgical treatment, he would not live.

Just like a hurricane, no one can predict the exact pattern or speed with which it will hit land. I could not predict what it would be like to arrive that evening at the Pediatric Intensive Care Unit. As I was being wheeled to the rear of the PICU, it felt as the eyes of every staff member were filled with pity. We were unprepared for the hurricane that was about to strike, and just like the person who stays behind despite the warnings to evacuate, I realized that this too was bad—very bad.

The PICU was eerily quiet. Not much noise besides faint, random beeping noises coming from other rooms—and whispers. No laughing, no crying. Just quiet. We turned the corner to get to Room 10, the isolation room. There he was, lying in an infant hospital bed with small plexiglass sides, high off the ground, hooked up to what felt like a million wires. But he was alive. He was stable and no longer needed the ventilator.

Devon Franklin, in a podcast with Oprah's Super Soul Conversations, said that we are in control of only two things: how we prepare for what might happen, and how we respond to what just happened. The moment when things happen—that belongs to God.[1]

Have you ever been in a situation such as these: working your tail off at a job that ended; having a lifelong friendship that suddenly stopped; striving for perfect health, only to find out you're terminally ill; or thinking that you were sailing through a class, when really you were sinking? All those moments for which you have taken all the necessary preparations, but somehow, they still don't go according to plan.

I couldn't control this situation. All the planning and preparations I had made were being whipped around in the winds of the hurricane, which hit me head on.

After just a short while, my body was exhausted, crumbling under the weight of emotional and physical strain. I couldn't communicate this to anyone because they would have made me leave him again. Then what? Will my baby think his mother left him? Did he even know I am his mother? Would he mistake the nurse for being his mother because he was looking at them for 12 hours a day? I could not leave him. Were it not for the loving influence of my husband, who wheeled me out so I could rest at the hotel across from the hospital despite my emotional indecisiveness, I wouldn't have found the strength to leave.

Because Alex was brought in on a Friday night, we were unable to speak with the doctor about his surgery until Monday morning. By Sunday, I was the walking dead. I was a wreck. Wrapping my head around all that was happening was shattering me emotionally, and my body was unable to function. I was pushing myself to walk as much as possible and stand next to his bedside as long as possible. I was propelling myself to a breakdown, and I needed to go home. The nurses prepared us for the long road ahead and encouraged us to get as much sleep as possible. After much deliberation, my parents drove me two-and-a-half hours home. I wanted to shower in my own shower, sleep in my own bed, and pack for the days ahead. My husband stayed back with his mom and stepdad and our precious little Alex. That night, I called to check on him. Instantly, I was jealous of my husband; jealous because he wasn't in pain from a surgery and was with our son when I wanted to be with him. A fear was ripping through me at this point because I was away from my baby and feared he wouldn't know I was his mother. Worse than that, what kind of mother *was* I? What kind of mother leaves her child two-and-a-half hours away because she wants to sleep in her own bed? *I'm not fit for this*, I thought. *I'm a horrible mother, a selfish mother.*

We awoke the next morning before sunrise to get to the hospital to meet with the surgeon. My father dropped off my mother and I at the door so I could be pushed in a wheelchair to his room. We rode up to the fifth floor and wound the corner to get to the PICU waiting room to be buzzed in. As I sat in the hallway leading to the PICU, my mother pushed the buzzer and told them, "Baby DeLeeuw."

The desk nurse replied, "They are in a family conference right now." I looked at my mother confused, did this mean I couldn't go back? My worst fear was coming true ... I was not considered his mother. They believed *I had caused all of this. They were not going to let me see him! They were making decisions without me because I was responsible. I had done this to him. They did not want me to know what I had done.*

Without me having to say a word, my mother quickly responded, "This *is* the mother of the child." They instantly buzzed us back. My mother wheeled me toward the room past the confused desk nurse. Then I saw my husband, my mother-in-law, and her husband all seated around Alex, along with a doctor who had drawn out diagrams and was wrapping up his explanation of the three-part surgery.

I was beyond angry at this point. I knew nothing about my son. I hadn't spoken once with a doctor. What was happening? Did they not want me to know? They were conspiring against me. They were making all the decisions without me. They were shutting me out.

I am sure the poor doctor thought I was a lunatic. Thankfully, he ended up not being our surgeon. Why else wouldn't the mother be there for such an important conversation? He must have thought I was unstable. He gave me a half-smile and spoke of keeping him monitored until we decided on a treatment plan. Then he walked out. The nurse reminded us that only two people at a time could be in Alex's room. My mother-in-law smiled and suggested Brandon accompany her and her husband to breakfast so that my mother and I could spend time with Alex.

I was livid and snapped back, "I haven't seen my husband since yesterday. So no, he is going to stay here with me."

When you are in a situation like this, the stress level is high and the tensions are higher. Things are said that normally wouldn't be said. People are reacting when they would usually brush it off. On a scale of 1–10, every emotion is at an 11. Not only that, but you are forced to sit in a waiting room (which was so incredibly tiny), and there is nothing anyone can do to fix the situation.

Over the course of the next few days, I learned the details of what was going on from my husband and our little boy's nurses. This hurricane was indeed projected to hit us head on, and we were not prepared for it. HLHS is a congenital heart defect that occurs in one in every 4,344 births.[2] With this heart defect, if the right side of the heart functions normally it can be modified so oxygenated blood can return to be pumped to the rest of the body. But in Alex's case as well as with all hypoplastic left hearts, the left ventricle (the "powerhouse" of the heart), was underdeveloped, as was the aorta, which could not send any oxygenated blood to the body. This severe type of heart defect should be detected on an ultrasound, as the two sides of the heart usually mirror each other in size.

We had no idea what to do but were given three options: let nature take its course and they would provide comfort for Alex;

wait for a newborn's heart by going on the heart transplant list; or undergo a series of surgeries. We were told that the surgeries would take place in the first few days (the Norwood procedure), between 4 and 6 months (Glenn), and the final surgery between 18 months and 3 years (Fontan).

After weighing our options, we decided to go with the three surgeries. The main purpose of the Norwood would be to "replumb" the heart and build a new aorta. They would use the pulmonary valve and artery to connect the old aorta to the new aorta. They would then remove the wall between the atria and insert an artificial shunt to maintain blood flow to the lungs.[3] Essentially, they were bypassing the left side of the heart and Alex would only be able to use the right side of his heart after the surgery. All this would be done to a heart the size of a walnut.

On the first of February, six days after Alex was born, we were surrounded by family and friends. Living several states away, our families left jobs, their own families, and even college classes to be our backbone of support. In the PICU, only two visitors could be in the room at a time. I held my little man for six hours straight as visitors cycled in and out from the waiting room. As I sat there looking at this sweet angel laying across my lap on a pillow, it was hard to fathom all we would soon endure and even harder to comprehend a six-day old undergoing open heart surgery. I was amazingly calm. I was aware of the complexity of the surgery, but I trusted our surgeon even though we had just met him, and I was positive the outcome would be great. As they wheeled him to the operating room, I walked as far as they would let me go and I looked into his eyes and told him, "Two weeks. We will be home in two weeks." Two weeks was our best-case scenario and I had to have hope that he'd be home in that time. I was pushing away any doubt deep inside.

More than six hours later, Alex was out of surgery and doing what they considered to be well. We were allowed to see him but were warned there were many people monitoring him. His chest would remain open to allow for swelling, and he was still on the ventilator. We were not allowed to touch him because it could startle him. We were met at the door by our smiling cardiothoracic surgeon, Dr. Andrew Lodge. He greeted us with a little university rival humor about Duke and UNC. This small joke eased my worry; this was the first time I had seen our surgeon relaxed. The surgery had gone well, and we were now playing the "waiting game" to see how Alex would do in recovery.

When a hurricane hits, it's not the up-to-date storm footage that captivates me. Sure, the winds are strong and the waves are high, but it's the aftermath of the hurricane that always sucks me into The Weather Channel. It is the flooding, the devastation, and the survivors that command my attention. All the preparations done by the town often are no match for a hurricane. The emotional toll on the people in the path of the storm is apparent. Those who wouldn't normally loot are grabbing things from shelves; survival mode.

The situation we faced with Alex's surgery is no different. Everyone is under emotional stress, feeling helpless. No one knows what to say and often what is said is misinterpreted by others. Not only are our words mangled, so are our actions. All the while causing a rift between family and friends, which may never fully heal. Just like a town ripped apart by a hurricane, we were in survival mode.

No warnings of what we were about to see could really prepare us for what it was actually like to see your newborn after open heart surgery. Before the procedure, he appeared stable and even healthy. He was not on a ventilator and we were able to hold him around the various lines to monitor and medicate him. But now, the number of lines going into his body and the ventilator down his throat was a lot for me to process. The scariest part was that his chest was open. There was just a thin film, similar to plastic wrap, over the opening in his chest and I could actually see his heart beating. Even though it's something that happens all day long, it was still difficult to see a beating heart. I could now see it with my own eyes, and it made my stomach churn. We were not allowed to stay for long, which, honestly, was fine with me. I needed time to process it all. This was much harder than I had imagined.

Oswald Chambers said, "Faith never knows where it is being led, but it knows and loves the One who is leading."[4] I was thankful to have entered this storm of uncertainty with faith. A faith that although loves to plan, isn't fearful of God's plans. Quite possibly, I still had the faith of a child. A faith that didn't fully understand how bad things could really get. I was naive, like those who choose to wait out a Category 4 Hurricane. I had no idea what was coming for me. One thing I did know was that if God had allowed me to see the whole picture and exactly where I was being led, I am positive I would have planted my heels in the ground and run the other way. Never would I have willingly entered this storm. Never would I wait out a Category 4 Hurricane.

In the early morning, we were awakened first by our cell phones—which I couldn't get out of bed fast enough to get—and then by the hotel phone. The nurse told us there was a complication, but that Alex was stable and we were to come to the hospital. She sounded calm and because I was still half asleep, I was confused. Brandon had a job interview that morning, so I proceeded to ask her if Brandon could come to the hospital after the interview. Her tone changed and she told me we both needed to go there now.

The word "now" woke me to the realization that it was not good. We frantically rushed around throwing on clothes and banging on my parent's hotel door. I'm not really sure what I wore to the hospital, but one thing is certain: I was probably a hot mess.

After being buzzed into the PICU, the doors automatically opened and I am not sure how they didn't just close on me. I was jarred from what I saw. At this point, Alex was in room 2, bed 1, which was directly across from the entry door. When the door opened, I was looking past the staff standing before us to lead us to our "family conference," and all I could see was the commotion around Alex's bed. Not only were there a lot people scurrying in and out of the room, there was the brightest light I had ever seen shining in his room. I couldn't help but think there were angels surrounding him, because the light was not like anything I had ever seen.

It seemed hectic and incredibly overwhelming. We were not allowed to see him but were instead immediately directed to the conference room. I will never forget the sense of urgency and fear I felt. It wasn't until this moment in time that I sensed I might actually lose my son.

In the conference room we sat at a large table. Dr. Lodge sat right next to us. His eyes were red, his face and body language rang loud and clear that he had done absolutely everything he could. Despite how clearly exhausted he was, he began to tell us what happened. Alex had gone into cardiac arrest. For 20 minutes he massaged Alex's tiny heart in his hand until it began to beat again. Alex was immediately placed on ECMO (a heart-lung bypass machine). This machine would circulate blood through an artificial lung back into the bloodstream, providing adequate oxygen and giving his heart a chance to "rest." We were told he should remain on this for a few days, at which point they would try to take him off the machine. The team did not want Alex to stay on ECMO for more than six to seven days. We were then allowed to see Alex.

I thought walking into the room after surgery was bad, but this was much worse. My little man looked horrific. The ECMO machine itself took up half of the room. He had two tubes of blood going in/out of his chest from this machine and two chest tubes draining blood. His chest was open, he had what looked like a magnet across his head tracking his brain activity, and he was still on a ventilator. I was in shock. All those episodes of *Grey's Anatomy* were no match for the reality of this point in time.

Alex was on ECMO for 13 days, almost a full week beyond the recommended time. While on ECMO, he was developing his little-fighter personality. I know it's hard to imagine that a baby who is just a week old has a personality, but he did. I would tell him I was going to eat or pump, and he would squeeze my finger (which was permanently placed in his right hand) and push out his bottom lip. That would always buy him at least 20 minutes before I would attempt to leave the room again.

On February 5th, my sweet husband bought me a slice of coconut cake (my favorite) from the cafeteria. We were celebrating two things: our one-year wedding anniversary and the baptism of Alexander Cole. Being raised a Catholic, Brandon was adamant about having him baptized. I've always believed that Jesus takes the children straight up to Him, but my husband's beliefs had him fearing the unknown. So, on this day, we dedicated him to a sovereign, loving, all-knowing God—believing that He had the best intentions for our son and for us, believing that our baby would indeed come home.

Eventually, family began to return to their homes, both near and far. Brandon returned to work, and my mom stayed with me. Every day we would get up early in the morning, drive two-

and-a-half hours to sit with Alex until the shift change and then would drive the two-and-a-half hours back home. I was blessed by her commitment and presence. She never interjected her opinions but would just listen. She was my rock. Over time, as my body began to heal and I began to realize "two weeks" was turning into a longer haul, I knew I needed to do this alone. I needed to live closer by moving into the Ronald McDonald House (RMDH). The problem was how to tell my mom. How do you ask your mom to leave when you know it will tear her apart? She will do it, but she will be brokenhearted.

Well I was a wuss and called my dad. He told her it was time to come home. I agreed and reminded her I would need her more when Alex came home and would need around-the-clock monitoring. As difficult as it was for her to leave, it was liberating to only have to worry about myself and Alex.

Throughout the next several weeks, Alex continued to fight for his life. He was placed on the heart transplant list because his heart no longer had the necessary elasticity to pump blood for a growing body. This was a difficult circumstance because you realize that in order for your newborn to receive a heart someone else has to lose a newborn. However, we did not let this affect our time with Alex. We had one rule and that was to stay positive. At no point was anyone allowed to cry around him. We wanted him to be surrounded by happiness and joy. I would read to him; sometimes gossip magazines, and we (well, me) would laugh at all the silly things people were worrying about. Alex knew all the scoop on Nick Lachey and Jessica Simpson. I would share stories of myself and his dad with the nurses so Alex could hear about how funny his daddy was. In fact, one day someone in the next room complained we were too noisy. We had started laughing and couldn't stop. One story led to another and another. Honestly, the complaint only made us laugh harder. Joy was what our son heard on these days. Deep belly laughter, love, and pure happiness was what surrounded his bedside. I like to think our laughter gave him the strength to keep fighting—this was my hope.

If I am being completely honest, I usually feel awkward in situations such as these. I am the person during a sappy movie laughing uncontrollably. It isn't because I have a heart of stone, but because when I feel the urge to cry around others, I can't help but laugh. I also didn't want to hold anyone else up. It is ironic because people come to visit you with the intention of "supporting you." The reality is many people couldn't handle seeing Alex. He was just a helpless child in a terrible situation. It was overwhelming to witness. Every visitor would walk through the door with a smile but would stop in their tracks when they saw him. There are no words to describe the cards he was dealt. If I didn't have the "no-crying-at-his-bedside" rule, I would have spent every visit comforting the person who visited. This was my reality, and I was spending enough time saying, "It's okay, we're okay," to everyone that wiping away tears didn't need to be on the list, too.

Most of the time it was just Alex, me, and a nurse. Brandon was two-and-a-half hours away maintaining the house and working so that we would have a home to bring him to. On his days off, Brandon would visit and stay with me at the RMDH. When he visited, it was always fun to see Alex's reaction. He would hear his daddy's voice and open his eyes so wide looking for him. He loved his daddy!

When your child is hospitalized or seriously sick you have to grasp on to any hope you have. You hope that the dreams you've envisioned for your child since you saw the positive pregnancy test still have a chance to come true.

Every Wednesday I would be filled with hope. Hope would

come when Edd Shope, the man who Life Flighted Alex, would visit to check on him. He would stay with me for thirty minutes to an hour each time telling me about his family, especially his children Maddison and Michael. He showed such great care and concern for us. I didn't realize just how valuable this time was until it registered how happy I would be to see him. The stories of his children were the distraction I needed. His friendship was a rare gift and I am so grateful for the time he invested in us. As another week goes by, more hope. Alex is still here.

With each passing day comes more faith. In his book, *Heaven is For Real*, Todd Burpo explains it simply: "Praying is afraid to hope; afraid not to."[5] Inside you are grasping for every gleam of hope. Yet you're afraid to hope or dream too much. You're even more afraid to walk away. Hope can be both terrifying and powerful.

When the "news breaks," you are swarmed by people. The generosity of others can actually be overwhelming. However, as time goes on, visitors are fewer and farther between. Just like the recovery of a hurricane, life does not stop for everyone else who lives in surrounding communities. Jobs, families, and activities don't come to a halt for everyone else. This reality can wear on your hope. You wonder, "Have we been forgotten?"

As I told you, I am a planner, so hope would also come in the form of routine. Day after day I would awake at the RMDH Durham, call the nurse, catch the bus to the hospital, and sit there next to him. I would rub his feet and run my fingers lightly across his face. I was even told by a nurse that I was spoiling him because I thought he had fallen asleep but, as soon as I stopped, he grimaced until I softly ran my fingers on his face again. I would arrive early and stay until I could not keep my eyes open any longer. I spent every waking second with my son. This was a time before texting was a big deal and there wasn't Facebook or even MySpace. I would make two phone calls every day during the shift change from 7–8 p.m.: one to my husband and the other to either my sister or mom. Sometimes I would venture to the Ronald McDonald Family Room, located on the same floor as the PICU, and send out a detailed mass email explaining his progress.

Max Lucado said, "Getting on board with Christ can mean getting soaked with Christ. Disciples can expect rough seas and stout winds."[6] How many times have the disciples dealt with rough seas? I can think of two actual encounters with rough seas (when Jesus was sleeping on the boat and He calmed the sea, and the other when He walked on water toward them). Numerous times throughout the disciples' lives they encountered people who threatened them and situations they couldn't control. Why should I expect anything less? The one thing the disciples knew was trust. This is where I was. I needed to trust. Hoping is trusting. I needed to trust God that He had my best interests in mind. When was the last time I felt the need to truly *trust*? I can't remember the last time I had been shaken to the core. I can't remember the last time I was afraid to this magnitude. I can't remember the last time I couldn't rely on myself. God was using this moment where I can't fix it, I can't plan it, and I can't control it. I had to *trust*. I needed to trust the prayer I prayed in the car the morning Alex was born that God would prepare our hearts for what was happening.

I am willing to get soaked in Christ. I am willing to be used. Lord Jesus, I am trusting you will heal my child.

You Say
Lauren Daigle[7]

You say I am loved when I can't feel a thing
You say I am strong when I think I am weak
You say I am held when I am falling short

CHAPTER THREE

THE HALLWAY
(THERE IS NO HOPE FOR HEALING)

A hallway may appear to be a passageway, but if you really think about it, you can probably vividly remember the feeling you had in a certain hallway. Maybe you grew up watching that creepy movie The Shining and you can envision the twins standing at the end of the hallway releasing a distinct fear inside you. Or maybe, like me, your parent's bedroom was at the end of the hallway and you knew no matter how long that hallway felt as a child, safety was at the end of it. Hospitals have hallways too, and this was where I would go to pray and recite scripture from memory. I am not sure if you have ever been in a place where you needed solitude, but this hallway became my safe place. It was where I could let my emotions be raw. I was often "alone," but here in the hallway, I could seek God's will unlike anywhere else. Maybe it was because by the time I got back to my room at the RMDH, I would be too exhausted to pray. In the room with Alex, I needed to be his strong momma and could only sneak in prayers. Here in this hallway, I could be vulnerable.

But Jesus often withdrew to lonely places and prayed.
Luke 5:16

In college, I went through a semester-long training program to become a Young Life leader, and during this time, we had to memorize scripture. Now, in the cold hallway of Duke Medical Center, this memorized scripture became my lifeline. I didn't have my Bible with me, and my flip phone didn't have the Bible App. It was Jeremiah 29:11 that I clung to day after day. On a piece of cut-up computer paper given to me by one of the nurses, I wrote it down and taped it above Alex's bed:

"For I know the plans I have for you," says the Lord. "Plans for good and not for evil. To give you a future and a hope."
Jeremiah 29:11

Having this verse above his bed reminded me that this was HIS plan. So many times, I felt paralyzed by fear: when we were told something was wrong; seeing his heart beating through the little piece of plastic; taking him off ECMO; and when they were finally able to close his chest. I know it sounds crazy that a closed chest could cause fear. The reality is when you get used to seeing his heart beating for three weeks and suddenly his chest was closed causing you to rely on a monitor to make sure it was still beating was scary. But each time, God was whispering to me: 1 But now, O Jacob, listen to the Lord who created you.

O Israel, the one who formed you says,
"Do not be afraid, for I have ransomed you.
I have called you by name; you are mine.
2 When you go through deep waters,
I will be with you.
When you go through rivers of difficulty,
you will not drown.

When you walk through the fire of oppression,
you will not be burned up;
the flames will not consume you."
Isaiah 43:1–2 (NLT)

I was in deep waters. I was in the rivers of difficulty. I felt like I could drown any second.

One afternoon, Alex's PICU roommate was undergoing a procedure, so I had to wait in the PICU waiting room until they were finished. As I sat there, I saw one of the "heart moms" I recognized walking out of the PICU and heading my way. She was visibly upset, shaken. When she saw me, she walked directly to me. In the doorway, she stood and told me they were taking her daughter off life support. Every parent's nightmare, letting her daughter go. I was shocked. Her posture showed defeat. Her words were that of courage. She described her daughter's suffering, the multiple times she had coded and been brought back to life and explained that she just couldn't do it to her daughter anymore. In an exhausted tone, she uttered "Why am I holding on?"

I got up from my chair and we embraced. As she walked away, I could only think of how selfless she was. Brave. And so strong.

Waters were rising. This was getting real.

In his book Sun Stand Still, Pastor Steven Furtick of Elevation Church said, "He's holding on to you ... As the big waves roll toward us, God promises to do the heavy lifting. He only requires that we have the faith to wade as deep as he leads and keep reaching up to Him."[1]

Live by faith. Trust in hope. Know that God is in control. As a plan-everything type of person, this whole scenario was pushing my limits. As you may recall, I was the one telling Alex,

"Two weeks, buddy. You have to do this."

Alex eventually stopped peeing, which at first we'd hoped was only temporary due to the cardiac arrest. We tried dialysis and it worked for a while, but only briefly. Alex was going to need a more permanent dialysis—my hope was being washed over by a big wave. The doctor assigned to do this operation came into our room with a team of interns. He discussed my child as if he were another "rat study" and I wasn't even there. Honestly, as a *Grey's Anatomy* fan, I know how a teaching hospital worked, so it wasn't until I listened to *what* he was saying that I got angry. Here is my child on full life support, and his body is swelling from toxicity; all the while they are debating the risks of operating on him. For the first time in all the weeks I was there, I spoke in anger. I told him if he doesn't take Alex, my son will die right here. I explained that our doctor already said he was getting it today. I then demanded he would operate because I would rather know he died in the operating room trying to save his life. When this doctor responded with, "I will discuss it with my team" and left the room, I broke all my rules and sobbed. I felt more helpless and hopeless than I had ever before. My child was sick, dying, and suffering and there was not a thing I could do about it.

I looked up to see my nurse through the window, eating lunch. In mid-bite she saw my tears, dropped her food, and came running in. She immediately called Dr. Lodge, who came to Alex's room shortly thereafter. Not only did Dr. Lodge reassure me that the surgery would happen that day, but he promised to accompany Alex to surgery and would be the one to keep me updated on progress. I wanted to hug him for this reassurance.

For me, this surgery was much more difficult emotionally than his open heart surgery. I was completely alone and less naive about what could actually happen. After I watched them wheel him away to the O.R,. I ran to the hallway. I could not get there fast enough.

Down this empty hall. Down on my knees. Down came the tears.

The tears of a terribly exhausted mom. I selfishly missed my bed, my husband, my dog, *my life*. I wanted a healthy child. I wanted to bring him home. I didn't want to do this hospital life anymore.

So here in this empty hallway, with my hands on the cold tile, I cried out, "Jesus! Jesus!" over and over again. I couldn't find the words. I was crying in fear, in pain for my son, and in complete exhaustion. The crying turned to ugly girl sobbing and my prayer shifted to, "Help me! Heal him! But I want *your* will, not my own."

He answered, "No, but you will be okay." The answer was clear. It was a loud whisper, and it was unmistakable. Whispering is intimate. Whispering is something that can only be done when you are close. He chose this moment to be clear and close enough to whisper. In this moment, in this whisper, I was able to see past the pain of my situation. I was able to see the heart of His plan. I then knew I had always known the answer, even before I knew anything was wrong.

I knew when I dreamed something was wrong.

I knew when we walked through the cemetery.

I knew when I cried out to God in the car the morning of my induction.

I knew when he was born.

I knew because all along God was preparing me in whispers. It was in the hallway where my heart knew what He was telling me all along.

The Lord is near to those who have a broken heart.
Psalm 34:18

6 Do not be anxious about anything, but in every situation, by prayer and petition, with thanksgiving, present your requests to God. 7 And the peace of God, which transcends all understanding, will guard your hearts and your minds in Christ Jesus.
Philippians 4:6–7

It was in the hallway where I had felt the peace Paul mentions in Philippians. So, instead of losing my mind, with this answer I knew each day after this moment would be a gift of time with my Little Man. I did not lose hope. My perspective of hope shifted. My focus shifted. I came to feel the way Peter did in Matthew 14:22–29.

22 Immediately Jesus made the disciples get into the boat and go on ahead of him to the other side, while he dismissed the crowd. 23 After he had dismissed them, he went up on a mountainside by himself to pray. Later that night, he was there alone, 24 and the boat was already a considerable distance from land, buffeted by the waves because the wind was against it.
25 Shortly before dawn Jesus went out to them, walking on the lake. 26 When the disciples saw him walking on the lake, they were terrified. "It's a ghost," they said, and cried out in fear. 27 But Jesus immediately said to them: "Take courage! It is I. Don't be afraid."
28 "Lord, if it's you," Peter replied, "tell me to come to you on the water."
29 "Come," he said.
Then Peter got down out of the boat, walked on the water and

came toward Jesus.
Matthew 14:22–297

Just as Peter was in deep waters, I was in deep waters. Just as the waves continued to crash into the boat, I was being rocked to my core. Just as Peter was terrified, so, too, was I. Just as Peter trusted Jesus to get out of the boat, so did I. God was calling me out; to step into this horrible situation where I could sink deeper and allow the waves to hit me.

It was in this moment that my focus shifted to Jesus. The situation around me could no longer shake me. The waves that wanted to pull me under had no power. I trusted in Him. I trusted He knew even if it was not okay, it would be okay. He was calling me and whispering to me to trust Him. To step out in faith. To keep my focus on Him.

With that, He provided a peace beyond description. How else do you explain why I could find joy during such a desperate time? Only He could keep me afloat in these waters.

> **Have you ever been here? Out in the middle of rising waters, surrounded by fear, pain, and the cycle of "what-ifs."**

After this, my husband and I were openly honest with the staff and told them we wanted to prolong Alex's life, but not his death. We asked them to please let us know when we were no longer prolonging his life, because we would have a hard time determining this.

Shifting our focus. God was allowing us more time. More time to soak in every detail of his face, his fingers, and his toes.

It Is So
Elevation Worship[2]

In the storm you are peace
And your love won't let me go
You have spoken
And I know that it is so

CHAPTER FOUR

THE CALM BEFORE THE STORM
(I CAN PRETEND TO BE OKAY)

Hope is Necessary in every condition. The miseries
of poverty, of sickness, of captivity, would without
this comfort be insupportable.
Samuel Johnson (1750)[1]

F or the next few weeks I rubbed Alex's face, held his hand, and massaged his cute little feet. It never really bothered me that I didn't get to hold him because I knew he needed to get better. On March 5th, the nurses blessed me with a wonderful gift: they allowed me to hold Alex. This was the first time I'd done so since his open heart surgery on February 1st. I had actually forgotten how abnormal all of this is until I got to do something "normal" like hold my child.

What a wonderful day this was and my best friend from Michigan, Amy, had come! It was a blessing for which I'll always be grateful, but it was also that unexpected splinter in your foot when you have already been struggling to walk. I realized, as I was uncomfortably holding my baby with wires and a ventilator across a pillow, that I will never hold him against my chest. I will never feed him a bottle and place his head up against my cheek to take in that sweet baby smell. I will never have those moments alone to rock and sing. It was gut wrenching.

Then the nurses encouraged us to do something else normal: go shopping. Neither Amy or I are shoppers nor was this something we did together, but they gently nudged (especially Amy) that this would be good for me. I never left the hospital and I needed to get out. While at the hospital I had realized comfortable shoes were a must with all the walking I would do each day just to get to him. So off we went with written directions, in a city we knew nothing about. You can guess it. We got lost. When we saw the airport, we were both looking at each other: "Didn't they say, 'opposite of the airport'"? The good news is we found the mall and picked out a pair of pink Nike Air shoes (that I continued to wear for the next eight years). The bad news is after we hit the high of finding the mall and finding shoes, we hit a low. Amy looked at me and said, "Do you feel a little guilty?" I responded with "Now I do!" We both low-key chuckled with a pang of guilt and hightailed it out of there *directly* back to Duke Medical.

As the days passed, I tried to hold on to hope. Hope that God will hear all the heartfelt cries of my family and friends who were all praying for Alex. I believed He would change His mind and use Alex's healing to glorify Him.

The second dialysis failed. He was filling with fluid, and the left side of his body was turning a purplish-red color.

Many nights I would stay until the early hours of the morning. It wasn't because I didn't trust the nurses, I did. It wasn't because I wasn't exhausted, I was. It was because I knew my time was limited. As time went on, I was clinging to every second. One of these nights, I distinctly remember it was 2:00 a.m., and Dr. Lodge rounded the corner. He was as shocked to see me as I was to see him.

He said, "What are you doing here at 2:00 a.m.?" I laughed and replied, "I am his mother. What are *you* doing here this late? Don't you ever sleep?"

I don't remember now why he was there so late, but I do remember appreciating his care. I did not feel like just another patient but that my son's life mattered to him. This gave me hope. Maybe, just maybe, a miracle was in the making.

On Monday, March 12th, Alex was fighting the ventilator. This was generally a "good" thing. But for me it was nerve wracking. I was worried about his swelling. I asked the nurse what would happen if he kept breathing over the vent and she said they would excavate him (remove the ventilator). Honestly, he looked so awful. I regretfully asked, "But will they be able to get it back in?" She answered openly and with pity in her eyes; she didn't know. I continue to press for information and asked if this means he would just suffocate. I didn't need an answer, her silence and the pain in her eyes was enough. I refocused on Jesus.

The waves were growing and the wind was hitting my face. The reality of this storm was making it more and more difficult to focus.

While sitting next to his bed and rubbing my fingers across his face, I prayed if God's plan was to take my son, He would make it clear. I prayed He would do this by failing another organ. I just needed to know what to do. The next morning, he was back on full ventilator support.

On Wednesday, March 15th, Edd came to visit me. It was a visit like most others, but this time, he stayed a little longer and told me even more stories about his son, Michael. The pride Edd had for Michael was so apparent. He told me about Michael's adventures and their golden retriever. Edd was the glimmer of hope to my week. His visits gave me a chance to take a breath and hear about life outside of this hospital. It was the friendship of someone I both admired and respected. We didn't know it yet, but this would be our last Wednesday visit.

March 17th was different from most mornings for me. With a jolt I woke up and felt an urgency to get to Alex. I rushed around my room at the RMDH and arrived at the hospital in record time. But he was fine, just a typical day.

My gut was right, it wasn't. I had the song, "Better Is One Day" playing repeatedly in my head. As I began to journal for the day, I wrote the words to the Matt Redman song.[2]

Better is one day in Your courts
Better is one day in Your house
Better is one day in Your courts
Than thousands elsewhere

I just kept thinking, better *is* one day to be in the Lord's presence. How can I ask my son to lie here suffering out of my own selfishness to have another day with him? In the middle of my journaling, the other cardiothoracic surgeon for the unit came into Alex's room. Although he introduced himself to me, I already knew him, as he was the surgeon for my friend Jamie's daughter. He then discussed Alex's condition with me as well as his prognosis. He was kind and to the point. He told me what I had felt all along. It was time. We had reached the point where fighting wasn't an option. He had lost full kidney function. The only thing they could do was a kidney transplant, but since he needed a heart transplant as well, his body would most likely not be able to sustain both transplants. We scheduled a family conference for the next morning. He told me he knew Dr. Lodge wasn't yet ready to give up the fight for Alex, but he also knew of our wishes to sustain his life and it was time to tell me. I thanked him, as I knew *"... better is one day."*

After hearing this, the nurse asked me if I would like to hold Alex. I sat there staring at my little boy who was losing the fight. Although I would give anything to take his place, I knew he was going to receive the ultimate healing. While I rocked him, Dr. Lodge walked in. He choked back tears as he discussed with me Alex's heart condition, his kidneys, and now his lungs as well. He informed me Alex's chest x-ray from two days earlier showed his lungs were doing well but today's x-ray showed that they were "wet" and deteriorated. Boom! An answer to prayer. I remember looking at Dr. Lodge and telling him it was okay. I knew he had done everything he possibly could and we would have a conference in the morning when Brandon got there.

There is something so impactful about seeing your doctor care about your child as much as you do. I will never forget the look in his eyes. I will never forget how I felt in that very moment: Confident in my answered prayer, confirmed from my hallway whisper, and respected from a doctor who genuinely cared about our family and my son's life.

As I sat there holding Alex, my nurse came back in the room. She said to me, "Edd comes and visits you often, right?" "Yes, he was just here a few days ago."

She bent down and looked me in the eyes, "Then I think you should know Edd's son Michael was in a boating accident yesterday and did not make it."

My first thought was *Michael is going to be waiting for Alex.* Then the emotion of it all hit me. Edd, the man who had given so much time, energy, and care for me was suffering. Michael was gone. My heart ached for his loss. I suddenly needed to get up. I had the nurse take Alex from my arms, and I ran out of there. The tears were welling up inside of me. How can this happen? How can God take away two sons, mine and Edd's? I wanted to call Edd. I wanted to reach out. Never have I experienced sorrow for the pain of someone else like I did right then.

The next morning, we had our family conference. Although, both Brandon and I felt oddly peaceful about it all, we still had tears running down our faces at the idea of "giving up." This was the first time I saw my husband cry. This whole time he had kept his strong face on. He had continued working so we would have a home when it was time to bring Alex home. He had kept facing each day knowing there was nothing normal about of it. I drew strength from his fortitude.

Later that night, before we left for the RMDH, my husband finally got to hold our sweet boy for the first time since the surgery, and I was beginning to struggle with the reality of signing the do-not-resuscitate papers. Just a few hours before, I ran into the mom of the child next door to us and told her we would be removing Alex from life support and I was saying goodbye. I envisioned this encounter to be similar to when the other mom had told me. I thought she would be supportive and remind me I was making a selfless choice. But this was not what happened. This mom questioned me. She questioned my faith and it began to fill me with doubts.

As my husband was holding our son, Denise, one of the advanced respiratory therapists, leaned over and whispered in my ear, "You and I both know if God wants him to breathe, he will." This was the best thing anyone could have said to me in this circumstance. She was right.

As the night wore on, it became more difficult to remember what Denise had said. As we sat on our bed in our room at the RMDH, we questioned our decision. Were we doing the right thing? Were we being selfish in some way? How do we actually *do* this? What if he begins gasping for air like they warned us may happen? How on Earth would we be able to handle that!? So, we prayed. We asked God if He would do two things: make it apparent when we walked into the room that we were doing the right thing and make Alex's death be peaceful.

My husband fell asleep soon after this prayer (how *does* he *do* that!). I slipped out of the room to sit in the wooden rocking chairs on the balcony where my friend Jamie was sitting. Jaime's mom and my mom had met in the waiting room of the PICU early in this journey. Her sweet daughter, Madison, was also born on January 26th and with a heart defect. We instantly bonded over our two little fighters. But this night was different. Although her daughter was still fighting, my son was going to be gone. She was a great friend that night because she did what any friend should do: she listened. She listened to me question. She listened to me cry. She made me laugh, as we both loved laughter more than tears. She listened to my fears and my sadness about leaving my hospital "family."

"Oh, child. Don't ever discount the wonder of your tears. They can be healing waters and a stream of joy. Sometimes they are the best words the heart can speak."[3]

The tears didn't stop flowing even as I passed out from exhaustion in the arms of my husband. I cried for all the dreams I was saying goodbye to. I cried for all the pain such a little boy had endured. I cried for the life he never got to live. I cried for every single memory I would never have.

The next morning, we walked into the room to see Alex. They had asked us to bring an article of clothing that he could wear on his last day that would still accommodate all the wires. This was the first time we saw him in clothes. Not just a diaper, but baby clothes. It was surreal. My baby was in a light green newborn gown with a stitching of a momma giraffe staring into the eyes of a baby giraffe. The only outfit he was to ever wear resembled my deep love and admiration for my child.

It was also hard to believe that he was even my child. He was so swollen he could no longer lift his arms or open his eyes. He had four-and-a-half liters of extra fluid in his body. Take that in for a minute: this is the equivalent of two 2-liter soda pop bottles of extra fluid in a seven-week-old's body. We knew then we were absolutely doing the right thing. Alex would no longer suffer. Thank you, Jesus, for answering our prayers.

Alex was then moved from our shared Room 2 back to his original room from the first night we arrived so we could have more than two visitors at a time to say goodbye. We were given the entire day to spend with him. He was heavily sedated so we could hold him without causing him discomfort. A few hours before we were scheduled to say our final goodbye, I was done with visitors. Remember, for so long it was just me, Alex, and a nurse. I am wired to be a hostess. I worried myself with everyone else's needs. I worried how others are feeling, doing, thinking and felt like I needed to support them. This was utterly exhausting, especially on a day such as this. I really wanted it to be just my husband and me with him. I understood others' desires to say goodbye and I wanted that for them, but at the same time, I wanted to be selfish. I knew that it was never going to be the same. I was never going to have these moments back. So, family and friends were asked to leave so we could have it like before. Quiet. Just the voices of mommy and daddy whispering to our son. Whispering our admiration. Whispering our love. Whispering every desire and dream we had been holding in our hearts. Never again would he hear our whispering. Never again would we be able to tell him how strong he was and how incredibly proud we were of him. He was our fighter. Our Little Man.

Many of the doctors and nurses became our friends and family in the seven weeks we were there. Because of this, we asked several of them to come be with us. Every single person we asked showed up. Some were just ending a twelve-hour day, some were just beginning, some were on their day off, but they came. We knew they would give us the support we needed without us feeling we had to support them. We knew just by having them in the room we would be able to focus on our last seconds with our son. This was one of the best decisions we made.

We played the Curious George soundtrack by Jack Johnson that one of the nurses had given us in his room. I sat on my husband's lap, and Alex was placed in our arms. They turned off all the machines (which, when you are used to looking at machines 24/7 was a little odd) and we closed our eyes as they removed his ventilator.

The instant I laid eyes back on my son I started crying because he was so beautiful. This was the first time I had seen his face without tubes and tape since he was born. After twenty minutes the song Lullaby[4] began to play.

> *Don't you cry, no don't you cry*
> *Sing this lullaby to yourself*
> *'Cause when I arrive dear it won't be that long*
> *No it won't seem like anytime that I've been gone*

Near the end of this song, Alex took his last breath. It wasn't frightening or gasping, it was like a sigh of relief. A sigh of relief from all the pain he had experienced during all those weeks. A sigh of comfort as he left our arms and woke in the arms of Jesus. A sigh of peace and our answer to prayer.

25 Jesus told her, "I am the resurrection and the life. Anyone who believes in me will live, even after dying. 26 Everyone who lives in me and believes in me will never ever die.
John 11:25–26(NLT)

One of our favorite doctors checked his heart rate and nodded with a tear in her eye; Alex was indeed gone. My husband and I both kissed him and placed him in his bed. We walked around thanking and hugging the staff we had grown to love like our own family as several of the nurses removed all the tubes, wires, IVs, etc., and cut his hair. We came back to his bed and whispered one last time. Gave one more kiss. Rubbed his sweet feet and fingers one final time.

In his book *Fearless*, Max Lucado says, "For those who trust God, death is nothing more than a transition to heaven. Your child may not be in your arms, but your child is safely in his."[5]

They handed us his lock of hair in a baggie. His first and last haircut.

Walking away was the hardest part of the journey so far. How do you walk away? How do you go knowing you will never return? It would never be the same. How do you just leave him lying there? How?

I honestly think I left quickly, knowing that if I didn't, someone was going to have to carry me out. I was completely broken. But I needed to be strong. I needed to pretend, even if it was just to get me to move my feet and get me out of the room, it was okay. I was okay. He was okay. If I can pretend I am just going to the RMDH for the night and returning in the morning, then maybe I can make it through the night.

Have you ever run away from what you feared the most?
Have you ever wondered what you would then become
without this one thing that has defined you: a job,
friendship, marriage, or dream?

But how am I mother without a child?

CHAPTER FIVE

DROWNING
(I AM ALONE)

But when he saw the wind,
he was afraid and, beginning to sink, Matthew 14:30

I awoke in a hotel room next to my husband with salted tear streaks across my face. It was all different. My routine was gone. My plan was gone. I was still trying to wrap my mind around the fact that my son was gone. It didn't feel like it was possible. How could this be?

When we returned to the RMDH to retrieve my things, it was hard to face the people there. It was hard to look around and know the "routine" that'd kept me sane had dissipated. The friendships I had built would be gone. I would never know what happened to 8 year-old Sarah and her brain tumor. I would not get to talk to 18 year-old Mabel while she awaited her double lung transplant. Their journeys were no longer a part of our journey. As I gathered up the last of my things, I could feel my chest tighten.

The tears rolled down my cheeks as we got into our cars to make the two and a half hour drive home. How can we return to the home we had prepared for our first child? How do we return to the home we bought because we found out we were pregnant? What do we do about the nursery we had decorated and all the baby things we had received?

One of the first things I noticed upon walking into our master bedroom was the baby bassinet my grandfather made for my birth had been removed from our bedroom and placed in the nursery. In fact, every reminder of a baby had been moved into the nursery. The nursery door was shut. It was as if I would be able to walk by this room and not remember exactly what it was set up for. This simple gesture, while done with good intentions, broke me.

But there was planning to do. I had to pull myself together and plan his funeral. When we moved to Robeson County, we were moving for a teaching job at Orrum Middle School. We had no idea this town with the middle school on one corner, the church on the other, and the General Store with the best burgers around was going to be such a blessing. Not only did my fellow teachers give me their sick days after my maternity leave ran out, along with gift cards for food and gas, they made all of the funeral arrangements. We didn't even know where to begin and lived sixteen hours from family. My boss made the arrangements for the funeral home to retrieve our son's lifeless body and told us where to go in the next few days.

When we arrived at the funeral home, we were embraced by a staff that was loving and kind. They helped us provide our son with a funeral service that was both unique and as cost efficient as possible. We knew we had medical bills totaling approximately $1 million headed our way. I wanted to see my son so badly, but at the time we had to wait until the viewing. As we began to finalize things and make cost decisions, we were told that a group of men who wished to remain anonymous were paying for the funeral. This was overwhelming and I found it difficult to understand why someone would do this for us. This gift was so unexpected and so incredibly generous. A giant weight had been lifted from our shoulders; we could breathe.

It was busy leading up to the funeral. I was in hostess and "get-crap-done" mode. Family and friends were coming in from Michigan, Indiana, Florida, and California. I didn't have time to digest what was really happening. My emotions could best be described as a roller coaster. I would be so busy I would *almost* forget. Other times I would be enraged. I didn't want the opinions of anyone else. I didn't want to know how others thought the funeral arrangements should go. I wanted Brandon and I to make all these final choices without the opinions of anyone else. This was it. This was all we would ever get to do for him, and I really didn't care what anyone else thought.

I distinctly remember a time when I lost it over this. I was sitting at the table working on Alex's scrap book that I insisted must be done so those who hadn't visited at the hospital could see his journey. (Side note: To the poor person at CVS who had to develop those pictures, check them, and then hand them to me, I am so sorry.) My husband was sitting innocently on the couch speaking on the phone taking in advice on the funeral arrangements facing away from me when I caught wind. It was like releasing a bull from the pen and my poor husband was the one waving the red flag, I went at him fast and furious. From behind, I jumped out of my seat and raced to the front of the couch. I then *paced* as I *ranted* about all these things I had been harboring regarding what I thought about other people's interjections on what we should do. My poor husband watched me with the look of a matador, know-ing he's about to get hit with the horns. He watched me pace for just a few laps, heard me, and spoke clearly into the phone, "I'm going to have to call you back." He slammed his flip phone shut, stood up and held me. He said then, "This is our son and we will do what we want." Oh, my Danny Zuko melted my heart.

The funeral is a bit of a blur. So many people came out to support us: family, friends, colleagues, and Duke staff. It is a lot like a wedding. Planning and preparation while engulfed with conversation, thanking every person for coming. Just like a wedding there is always the one person you didn't anticipate to show up, but does anyway. There is also the person who makes a remark you could have lived without hearing. It was in the receiving line when someone asked me why we were not going to a burial site. I informed this person we were not burying him but having him cremated. The utter shock on this man's face was my first cue of his disapproval. But he did not stop there. He continued to tell me why I should have him buried. It took all of me to control my words, keeping them at bay.

Then it was all over. All our family traveled home and everyone else returned to their normal lives. There was nothing left to talk about. There was no news to share. There was no more "to-do" list.

Here we were, left alone. I was broken. I was hopeless. The waves that had been surrounding me all along now felt bigger. I was being pulled under.

I have always had a fear of drowning. I am not afraid of the water but the potential struggle in the water. Maybe it is the "made-for-TV" drowning that scares me; the struggle to keep your head above water, violently splashing, gasping for air, the unheard cries for help, and then slipping under. In actuality, drowning looks nothing like that. Instead it is usually silent. There is no waving or crying out for help, no focus, and it often goes unrecognized.

That's how I felt. I may not have been physically drowning in water, but I was being pulled under and I didn't want anyone to know.

Every single part of me hurt. I can't even begin to count the number of times I paced the house not knowing what to do, or how many nights I laid in my bed unable to close my eyes despite how exhausted I was.

The countless number of nights I walked out my front door in my pjs, shoeless and contemplating just walking off. I specifically remember looking down at my socked feet with my toes hanging over the brick steps. *If I just walk away right now, leave this all behind, and disappear, it can be over. Someone take me. Someone kill me. Take me from the darkness.*

Darkness does things to you. Darkness makes pain hurt more and crazy thoughts often run wild. It's amazing how these same crazy thoughts can appear surreal in the daylight, but at night reality. If I did manage to fall asleep, I would wake up to a baby crying; only to realize there was no way it was possible. I would then go to Alex's room and sleep on the nursery rug in front of his crib. I ended up having to get an over-the-counter sleeping pill. I would lay there and consider taking the whole box; thankfully, I have never been able to swallow pills, so I couldn't fixate too long on this thought.

When the morning would finally come, I wouldn't want to get out of bed because doing the simple day-to-day things was hard. Food had no taste. Doing what should be normal felt wrong. I would sit in the shower sobbing until the water turned cold, even then it wouldn't really matter. Nothing mattered. What really mattered was stripped from my arms.

I would sit in his untouched nursery and rock in the glider smelling the only outfit he had ever worn alive. The worst of my depression occurred when school was released for the summer and I no longer had to report anywhere. My husband had left for work with me sitting in Alex's nursery. When he returned from work, I was in the same place and honestly couldn't tell him if I had moved or not. It was then he called in the reinforcements, my mother. She was a nice break, but she couldn't stay forever.

I was so wrapped in pain, I struggled with reality. If you let yourself fall in depression, you will slip fast. If you let yourself dwell in self-pity for even a day, it will turn to months. I was like Peter I had lost my focus. I could once walk toward Jesus but now the reality of the waves was too much.

Satan wanted to isolate me. I isolated me. It was easier. I didn't have to pretend and put on a smile. I didn't want to laugh or show happiness because did that mean my heart was cold and I was moving on too quickly? I couldn't talk to my friends and family about it because no one really understood how I felt and besides, I was *supposed* to be getting better. I didn't want to burden them with all my pain, when I knew it just made them feel helpless.

My husband and I were grieving completely differently, and I couldn't talk to him either. He didn't want to talk about it. He instead converted our carport to a garage and added a fence to our yard. He was able to physically work through his grief. I couldn't burden him with my own struggles when he was trying to make it through, too. If we still lived in Michigan I would have without a doubt, just gone home to my parents. There is something about "going home" to your parents that feels good. If I would have been able to do that, it would have broken us. Michigan was sixteen hours away, so we were forced to see each other. We were forced to figure it out together. The myth is that when you lose a child you can lean on each other because you are experiencing the same loss. Unlike when one loses a family member or a close friend, both will carry grief but will still be able to hold the other up. It is hard to grieve the same loss so differently. You can't hold each other up. It is not fair to put your grief on the other person. We both carried our own shame and regret. We had different upbringings and different ways to cope. There was nothing easy about navigating these untraveled waters. We had to learn to be patient, to listen, to give each other space, and to cling to each other.

I was spiraling out of control in my own mind and was angry everyone else could move forward while I couldn't. This was just the tip of my anger. Why I was really angry was because I didn't know what I had done to deserve this! I tried to do things "right." I didn't party in college; instead, I spent my four years as a YL leader, sharing the gospel with teenagers. The reason my husband and I got married so quickly is because I had been offered a job in North Carolina. Originally, we were going to live together until our already-planned-and-paid-for wedding in June. My heart and soul couldn't do it. I knew it was not what God wanted for me. We quickly planned a small wedding before we moved. I was really trying. Wouldn't God *bless* our marriage and life for this?

For you created my inmost being; you knit
me together in my mother's womb.
Psalm 139:13

How could this be? How could a loving God have created my son to die? Why would God do this to me? I felt betrayed. Betrayed by a God whom I had believed in His love for mankind. Betrayed by a God who was supposed to be good. This was not good. The pain I was experiencing was not good.

Have you felt betrayed by God?

Living in the South, where there is a church on every corner, I received well wishes from people who meant well, but their words didn't help. Every time someone would tell me "God doesn't give you more than you can handle," I wanted to scream out to them. "Really?!?! Because *this* I can*not* handle! So, you are wrong!" Instead, I would put on my best fake smile. My favorite remark from others was, "You're young, you can have more." As if *that* would make me feel better.

I would force myself to go to church. I didn't want to worship a God who would do this, so I would spend most of the sermon rebuking everything the pastor was preaching, thinking *Yeah, well if you knew what I knew…* Often I would ask the pastor why God would allow this to happen. They would never have a good answer. Then we would try a different church.

I was supposed to be this strong Christian. All the emails I sent asking for people to pray. What would people say if I showed brokenness? I needed to stand firm in my faith, even if it was fake for everyone else. The old saying, "Fake it until you make it," was my motto. I was going to fake it, but whether I would make it was questionable.

One summer afternoon, I opened the mail and found myself looking at a birth/death announcement of Alexander, my Alex. It was confusing because I had not made them and yet, it was of my child. It was not a box for me to send out but a single announcement sent to me. It was beautiful, but it was painful. It was painful because, in this I realized I had nothing. Every single thing I knew I would do when my child arrived had been stripped from me. Every dream disappeared. Everything was gone. Alex would never come back. He was never coming home.

Then I did what no grieving mother should do: I went to Walmart. Walmart is one of the great places where anyone can fit in regardless of clothing choice. In every Walmart across the country you are greeted with the sounds of kids whining/crying while their parents are losing their patience. There in the cereal aisle I saw a tired momma. Her newborn was in a car seat in the cart crying while her toddler was running around grabbing things. She was losing it. She grabbed the toddler by the arm and jerked him to the cart. I stopped and stared. I realized I wasn't really even a Momma anymore. It was taken from me. I didn't choose this, but she still has her babies! I wanted to scream out, "Just love them! You don't know what you have!" Instead, I abandoned my cart there in the aisle and ran to my car. It seemed the entire world was ungrateful for life.

This season in my life forced me to realize all the shame I carried.

I had not been strong enough- shame.

I didn't have enough faith in his healing- shame.

When I could laugh again- shame.

When I would find joy- shame.

Whenever I thought about "moving on"- shame.

When I wasn't able to "move on" fast enough for everyone else's timeline- shame.

When I made people cry because of harsh words I spoke out of the pit of my pain- shame.

For not wanting to live anymore- shame.

For wanting to live- shame.

For wanting to turn my back on my faith- shame.

WHY GOD?? Why would you betray me? I trusted you.

For three years, I had prayed the prayer of Jabez.

*Jabez called upon the God of Israel, saying, 'Oh that you would
bless me and enlarge my border, and that your hand might be
with me, and that you would keep me from harm so that it might
not bring me pain!' And God granted what he asked.*
1 Chronicles 4:10

I did see you enlarge my territory. I did see you allow
conversations to unfold. I did see these things, but where was the
protection from harm and pain when I needed it the most?

In John 11 we read,

*There was a man named Lazarus, brother to
Mary and Martha, whom God loved that was very sick.*

In verse 3, the sisters send word that he is sick. But Jesus
does not go to them. Lazarus dies. When Jesus finally gets there,
Lazarus has been gone for four days.

*20 When Martha heard that Jesus was coming, she went out to
meet him, but Mary stayed at home. 21 "Lord," Martha said to
Jesus, "if you had been here, my brother would not have died.*

I can't help but think that Martha was out seeking an answer from Jesus, while Mary was so angry and stricken with grief
that she chose to seclude herself. Martha is the "get-crap-done"
person. When she sets her mind to finding out something, she will.
Martha wanted to know why he didn't come. I can hear her plead
as her voice trembled. It was so hard to understand how a loving
God would just choose to not show up; choose to not heal.

32 When Mary reached the place where Jesus was and saw him, she fell at his feet and said, "Lord, if you had been here, my brother would not have died." 33 When Jesus saw her weeping, and the Jews who had come along with her also weeping, he was deeply moved in spirit and troubled.

I hear myself in Mary. In every voice crack, in the weeping, in the position of being on her knees. I hear myself in her cry, "if you had been here." This is how I feel. Why didn't you come? You could have. You knew. Why did you choose this?

Jesus's response: he was deeply moved in spirit and troubled. Another version says, "*he groaned in the spirit"(KJV)*. God doesn't want us to experience this pain. This is why he used this moment to bring Lazarus back to life, to show a physical example of His coming death and resurrection.

Unlike Lazarus, He didn't bring back my Alex. Although I have hope in knowing because of Jesus' resurrection, Alex and I will see each other again in heaven, it didn't fix the fact I am still here. Here without my son. Here alone, trying to understand.

I did not want to do this anymore. Slowly I was letting go. Slowly I stopped battling the waves. Slowly I let my lungs fill with water. Soon I would be completely under without a sound. No one would know.

The Weepies
World Spins Madly On[1]
Woke up and wished that I was dead
With an aching in my head
I lay motionless in bed
I thought of you and where you'd gone
And let the world spin madly on

CHAPTER SIX

THE LIGHTHOUSE
(NOT ENOUGH)

G oing from being a Michigan girl to a North Carolina girl, I have always loved lighthouses. They line the beaches all along the Great Lakes. As a child, they were something that was a part of the scenery, nothing that stood out as unique. As I got older, I realized not only their beauty and uniqueness, but their importance. I love how they have different marks for the day (paint color) and night (light pattern), and each lighthouse is unique to the landscape and the beach it protects.[1] I love the history of them and how they help warn sailors of the danger ahead and guide them back home.

I can't pinpoint exactly when things started getting better for me, but one thing I did that was so helpful was read. I read book after book of other mothers who lost their children. For me this was comforting. I knew I wasn't alone. I could read about someone else's experiences and know that, although I felt like I was losing it, I was okay. Other people have gone through this too in their grief. I read about how couples grieve differently, and because of this, there is a high percentage of marriages that end in divorce. I was determined for this not to be us!

After several weeks of diving into literature on grief, I was reminded of the hallway whisper at Duke Medical. That moment when God called me out into these waters. To trust him. I had lost my focus on Jesus and like Peter in Matthew 14, I was drowning.

30 But when he saw the wind, he was afraid and, beginning to sink, cried out, "Lord, save me!" 31 Immediately Jesus reached out his hand and caught him. "You of little faith," he said, "why did you doubt?" 32 And when they climbed into the boat, the wind died down. 33 Then those who were in the boat worshiped him, saying, "Truly you are the Son of God."

This *is* when I realized I just needed to reach out my hand to Jesus. He was waiting for me all along. He was not going to let me drown, but I am also free to choose. Because of this freedom He gives us, I had to reach out my hand to be pulled up. Look again at verse 31:

Immediately Jesus reached out his hand and caught him.

It doesn't say "and then sometime later" or "after he begged." No, it says "immediately." This is truth. This is truth because I lived this. All the other times when I was talking to God, I wasn't asking for help. I was crying and yelling *at* Him. I was asking Him why and I was angry. But not once had I asked for His help. I was too engulfed with the waves around me to remember all I needed to do was reach for Him. Even in the instances when I was angry with Him and yelling at Him, He never left me. He was waiting for me.

Just like a sailor lost at sea or fighting the dangerous weather, I needed to set my eyes on the light. I needed something stable and constant. Something the wind and waves can't alter. A light pattern just for me to find my way back to the shore. Jesus is my lighthouse.

I have talked often of how I am a planner to my core. My heart cries for consistency and well-planned everything. I find peace in the rhythm. In Isaiah 55:8–9, it says

8 *"For my thoughts are not your thoughts, neither are your ways my ways," declares the Lord. 9 "As the heavens are higher than the earth, so are my ways higher than your ways and my thoughts than your thoughts."*

I have heard many pastors talk about perspective. I get so caught up in the right now, the what is right in front of me, that I often forget there is so much more. God's perspective is different because He can see it all. He sees more than the right now. He knows the outcome of my pain.

So I did what I do best. I began praying again and started planning. I planned to get up every morning. I planned to get dressed and make my bed. I learned quickly that a made bed was far less tempting to crawl back into. I planned to go to work. I planned to remember my Little Man and to make him proud. It sounds simple, but it was often extremely hard to do. Each day got a little easier. Each day a little brighter.

Then we began planning traditions. For the first Christmas following Alex's death, we got the grandparents gifts that incorporated Alex, knowing they were grieving as well: a silver booty ornament engraved with his name. For his first "angel day" we each wrote him a note, attached them to balloons, and released them. We felt this was a great representation of him leaving this Earth and reaching farther than we could see.

Sometimes the morning starts out bright and the skies

appear clear. Then you are reminded with a noise or a smell that can take you right back. A smell that can literally bring you to your knees, paralyzing any further movement because you are back in the hospital room. For me I don't want it to go away. I want it to stay. For just a brief moment I can see Alex laying there, every little wrinkle in his chubby arms, the pulse oximeter burning a red light wrapped around his foot. I can see his fingers wrapped around my index finger. I can lean into the fold of his neck, and whisper into his ear "I love you." The smell dissipates and I am left behind. This is when the fog sets in. Sometimes the fog can clear relatively quickly when I can say, "Thank you God for that. Thank you for sending me a reminder. Thank you for letting me *see* him again."

Other times I am triggered by reminders of all that I will never get to do with him.

Never kiss his head before his first day of school.

Never hear him tell me he loves me.

Never hear him say "momma."

Never see him fall in love for the first time or catch him after his first heartbreak.

Never get to dance the mother/son dance at his wedding.

Never get to see him hold his first child.

The fog can sometimes roll in so slowly you don't even realize it has been coming in. You know you are irritated. You know something is off, but you're unsure why. A birthday, the angel anniversary date, Mother's Day, Father's Day, or Christmas can all just come out of nowhere, but subconsciously, you are struggling with it. Suddenly you realize you are in this funk and the fog is all around you.

In the beginning, the fog would come in the form of anger. Time and time again, we found people using our son to bring themselves some sort of pity from others. They would share with others as if they were the ones sitting with me day in and day out, when most often they only visited once. They would do things in "his memory" without asking for our permission and we would only find out after it happened. This was hurtful. Not once did Brandon and I want anyone's pity. We wanted only to love our son and fight for his life. Even after losing him, I felt an overpowering need to be strong; to not be in a "victim mentality." I never liked feeling pitied. I only want him to be remembered.

This rolls into the next wave of fog- the fear of forgetting. First it was my own fear. Will I remember every wrinkle, every lip pout, every tiny toe, the scrunching of his nose, every little detail? Then this evolved into, Will he be forgotten by the world? How can a child so little be remembered? How can his life have meaning?

Again, this fog only lasts a short while. It is the words of others that linger longer, placing a thickness that is hard to push through. One day about four years after losing Alex, a small town pastor who barely knew me and wasn't around when Alex was sick, had heard of Alex's story from his wife and found it necessary to share with me his beliefs. I was out taking a walk when he stopped me to tell me I didn't have the "right hands" praying over him. He said if I would have had the right hands praying over him and *faith*, Alex would have been healed.

I walked away shocked and in disbelief. I was so angry that he would tell me this. First of all, who are these "right hands"? Elders or a group of sinful humans who can apparently get more communication from God than just my normal self? I was outraged. The worst part was that he planted in me a seed of doubt. Did I not pray hard enough? In my hallway whisper I believed in God's comfort and peace, knowing that his answer was "no," but should

I have demanded healing? Was God testing me to push and pray for this healing?

This fog of doubt is the worst kind. Quickly, I can no longer see my lighthouse pattern. So as any waves increase, I can't stay focused. I can't stay above the water. I begin swallowing water. Even the smallest of waves feels overwhelming when I can't see and I'm taking it in.

Brandon's sister had a son just a few months after Alexander and this would crush me in the fog. On a clear day I am happy for her, but on a day when every wave is going over my head like a skip on a scratched cd, I can't handle it. Several months after Alexander passed away, Brandon's grandparents had their 50th wedding anniversary. I couldn't bring myself to go. I absolutely adore them, but I knew I couldn't be around my newest nephew yet. Even as he grew older, I would see him and know our son would be the same age. I wonder what Alex would be doing. And in the thickest of fog I cry out "Why us?" I am aware it is completely unfair, but when the waves are rising I can't help but gasp for air, and with that, anything rational is nonexistent.

I find myself crushed under the weight of this fog, completely blinding me from seeing the perspective of Christ spoken in the Book of Isaiah. When I remember God doesn't think the way I do, nor does He act the way I do, I am humbled. I am not to understand an infinite God. As frustrating as this may be at times, I will not be able to see the full picture.

Max Lucado said, "Satan keeps you and me from prayer. He tries to position himself between us and God."[2] Satan absolutely uses the fog to position himself. So, in the fog, I try to follow James 4:7–8

7 Submit yourselves, then, to God. Resist the devil, and he will flee from you. 8 Come near to God and he will come near to you.

Every day I have a choice. I can either allow the fog to restrict my vision and then drown in anger, doubt, and destructive thoughts, or I can find my hope and light pattern on the horizon. Just as many lighthouses have now become quaint tourist attractions rather than life-saving necessities, so too can my faith.[3] I can pretend it's lifesaving or I can allow it to actually *be* lifesaving.

My Lighthouse
Rend Collective[4]
In the silence, You won't let go
In the questions, Your truth will hold
Your great love will lead me through
You are the peace in my troubled sea, oh oh
You are the peace in my troubled sea

CHAPTER SEVEN

THE RAINBOW
(MY SHAME DEFINES ME)

I am really not sure how Edd Shope and I got back in contact with each other, but when we did, I got to speak with his wife, Tamma. They were such a blessing for us. They were a couple that was going through all the "firsts" with us. Someone I could call who truly understood me. Never would they try and make it better. They understood there was nothing to fix, I only needed to be heard and so did they.

In early 2007 we discovered we were having another boy. Brandon and I both knew we wanted to honor Edd and Tamma by naming our son after Michael. We decided we would name him Xavier Michael. Just as we never want Alex to be forgotten, we want Michael to be remembered, too. Every time we tell anyone Xavier's name, we are able to tell the story of Michael. When Xavier turned 3, Edd and Tamma came to his birthday party and Xavier held up his hand to show them he was three. However, when Xavier does a three, he always puts his thumb and index finger together to hold up the remaining three fingers; so did Michael. Years later when Edd and Tamma came to watch Xavier play soccer, Tamma noticed Xavier's orange cleats. Orange is one of Xavier's choice colors; it was Michael's too.

After a storm when the sun comes back out you will often see a rainbow. My rainbows after this journey were the births of Xavier and our daughter, Irelyn. They in no way replaced Alex, but they did fill my empty arms. They did bring back sunshine, smiles, laughter, and all the blessings of raising babies. All the traditions we had started became much sweeter with them. Growing up, I had a friend whose brother passed away. I remember playing at her house one day and asking whose baby picture was on the wall in the living room. She stopped, frozen, and whispered, "That is my brother. He died when he was a baby, but we don't talk about him. It makes my mom cry." I remember wanting to ask questions. I didn't know babies could die, I thought only old people did. I also remember feeling sad they couldn't talk about him. This memory has stuck with me, and I knew I didn't want my children to feel this way. I knew I wanted them to be able to speak freely of him and to be able to include him. We share with our children who their brother is. We do not hide pictures, even the "bad" ones. We are honest with them about how Alex was born with a bad heart and was really sick.

Now, for Alex's birthday, we celebrate. This has gotten easier over the years. Together we bake a cake or cupcakes and have a celebration. In the past we have gone to different kids' museums, play places, and even stay overnight at Great Wolf Lodge. We will go to dinner and just do something fun. We often have our closest friends come and celebrate with us. We are always amazed that even though they never met him and we didn't become friends with them until years later, they are willing to do this. These are true friends. True friends celebrate with you and when they see your eyes fill with tears, they nod to you because they recognize your pain. They don't make it a big deal or make you feel less for the emotions you still carry. They just exhibit they "see me" and will never forget him.

For the first eight years we also remembered his "angel day." We would do this by releasing balloons. The number of balloons represented the number of years he had been gone. We each would write him a note, including the kids, attach it to the balloons and release them. The kids loved sending notes to heaven.

For the 5th anniversary in 2011 we met Edd at Duke Medical Center. He took us up to the roof to see and get in the helicopter and then down to see the ambulances. Our final stop was to the new Pediatric Cardiac Unit to visit the nurses. As we were standing there in the unit, a little girl fully dressed rolled by in a wagon with her mom, grandma, and a nurse. Her port was under her clothes and looking at her you would not know there was anything wrong with her. Xavier, then four, watched her pass us and pulled on my hand to come to his level. He looked me in the eyes and whispered, "Mommy, that little girl is really sick."

I said, "I know, buddy."

He looked at me with a plea in his eyes and said, "No mommy. She is REALLY sick." I just nodded and continued to speak to the nurses. A few minutes later Xavier started yelling for Alex to come back and he wanted to see his brother. We all stood there frozen and with tears welling in our eyes as we looked at each other.

Edd, scooped up my then frantic child and said, "I'll take him to see the fish."

On the drive home we asked Xavier what his favorite part of the day was, assuming he would respond with the helicopter or ambulances. He said, "Seeing Alex." We didn't understand this response. We thought he was confused thinking maybe one of the children in the unit was his brother.

A week passed and on the way home from church Xavier

is talking to his sister in the car. Irelyn says, "Plane."

Xavier responds to her, "Cars not fly. Planes do. Helicopters do. Alex do too." Brandon and I just looked at each other. Neither of us knowing what to say.

The little girl's mom we saw at Duke Medical Center and I became Facebook friends. I began praying for their sweet little girl, Korah, praying for a different outcome. However in May, not even two months later, she had a brain bleed and had to be removed from life support. I knew the pain of this mother and I was again finding myself frustrated with God.

That night, before bed, I was rocking the kids and thinking about Alex and trying to focus on Christ as my lighthouse, thanking him for my little rainbows in my lap. Xavier says, "Me wish Alex could come back."

I said, "Me too, buddy."

He looked up at me and said, "But he's not sick no more." All I could say while holding back from sobbing was, "No, he's not."

I was chosen. God chose me to give love. He knew Alex would only need one thing from his parents and that was love. God watched over me. He blessed me with this sweet boy that taught me more about love than any "normal" child could have. He taught me about how much we take for granted every single day. We are lucky to be chosen to be his parents.

"As a mother comforts her child, so will I comfort you;
and you will be comforted over Jerusalem."
Isaiah 66:13

A few days later I decide to have a conversation with Xavier being more intentional, as best as you can with a four-year old, about Alex.

"Hey Xave who is Alex?"

"My brother. He isn't sick."

"He isn't?"

"No, not no more."

"How do you know him?"

"Me saw him."

I begin choking back tears, "You did?! When?"

"At the hospital."

"Where in the hospital? At the helicopter?"

"No"

"At the ambulance?"

"No."

"In the room where his friends are?"

His whole face lights up, "Uh huh!"

"What did he look like?"

"Not sick. Then he went with God and I cried for him to come back. Can I go play now?"

I probably sat there stunned for thirty minutes. Is this true? He did cry that he wanted to see Alex and he wanted him to come back. How did he see him and I didn't?

I have heard of others speaking of reminders from their loved ones. Edd always sees geese flying in a V (this even happened at one of the Xavier's soccer games when they came to watch) and finds dimes. For me it comes in a certain smell, the mention of his name, and not often but sometimes I will see a glimpse of a child's hand or a blonde little boy that will then vanish. The first time I experienced this it startled me. My parents found a misshapen heart rock on the beach the day he died. Since then, they always find them. One summer we were all getting together on the beach in Michigan for a family picture. I had intended to bring his footprint mold to place in the sand to be with us. When I discovered I had forgotten it at home in North Carolina I was overcome with grief. How could I have forgotten my child? As my mom was comforting me, my grandmother walked up with a heart shaped rock my grandfather had found. She was so happy that he had given this to her, but my mom and I were thinking of Alex. Then my four nieces came running toward us. They had *each* found a heart shaped rock and they knew the significance. This was huge because not only has the heart shaped rock never been found on a Michigan beach, but now we were holding five heart shaped rocks and he would have been five years old. I don't believe this was Alex, but I do believe they were reminders from heaven that he is ok and a reminder that I am ok.

With time our grief has changed so has our need to do certain traditions.

Although we have created many little traditions over the years, the most important thing we do is talk about Alex. Now our kids have taken on the ownership of raising money for the American Heart Association each year. Their goal every year is to raise $100 for every year of his current age if he were still with us. They make phone calls and go door to door to neighbors. Every year they surpass their goal with pride. The have even received plaques for being top fundraisers in the state of North Carolina.

Even with all the joy we have from our little rainbows, sometimes it is just hard to understand why.

When I am asked how many children I have, there is always a hesitation. Do I include all of them but then have to explain the one who is missing? Inevitably the person will ask where the missing child is. This will lead to the "pity look." I will need to then respond quickly with "it's ok." Often times this leads to awkward conversations. Sometimes, it feels as though I am seen as holding on too long to something I should let go. The other option is to not mention Alex at all. If I choose this I am choosing to deliberately forget his existence only for my own selfishness to avoid the awkward conversation. It feels like a battle I can never win.

God has never promised me a life free from pain.

> *Yes, and everyone who wants to live a godly*
> *life in Christ Jesus will suffer persecution.*
> *Timothy 3:12*

When I read this before I always considered it persecution from non-believers. Now I can get wrapped up in the "what did I do to deserve this?" As I have been studying Peter, I have come across this in Luke 22:31–34 (NLT)

> *31 "Simon, Simon, Satan has asked to sift each of you like*
> *wheat. 32 But I have pleaded in prayer for you, Simon, that*
> *your faith should not fail. So when you have repented and*
> *turned to me again, strengthen your brothers."*
> *33 Peter said, "Lord, I am ready to go to prison with you, and*
> *even to die with you." 34 But Jesus said, "Peter, let me tell you*
> *something. Before the rooster crows tomorrow morning, you*
> *will deny three times that you even know me."*

Peter tends to be confident in his faith, some would even use the word arrogant. Even so much as to say he would die for him. I too was confident in my faith. Never before had my faith in Jesus been rocked. I was born into a Christian home, attended Sunday School, Vacation Bible School, a parochial school, and then in college was a YL leader and active in my church. I *knew*

God. I believed in a good, good Father.

Jesus says Peter will be sifted like wheat. For wheat to be sifted it must be vigorously shaken in a sieve. The wheat kernels needed to be separated from the debris; sorting the valuable from the worthless.

54 So they arrested him and led him to the high priest's home. And Peter followed at a distance. 55 The guards lit a fire in the middle of the courtyard and sat around it, and Peter joined them there. 56 A servant girl noticed him in the firelight and began staring at him. Finally she said, "This man was one of Jesus' followers!" 57 But Peter denied it. "Woman," he said, "I don't even know him!" 58 After a while someone else looked at him and said, "You must be one of them!" "No, man, I'm not!" Peter retorted. 59 About an hour later someone else insisted, "This must be one of them, because he is a Galilean, too." 60 But Peter said, "Man, I don't know what you are talking about." And immediately, while he was still speaking, the rooster crowed. 61 At that moment the Lord turned and looked at Peter. Suddenly, the Lord's words flashed through Peter's mind: "Before the rooster crows tomorrow morning, you will deny three times that you even know me." 62 And Peter left the courtyard, weeping bitterly. Luke 22:54–62 (NLT)

Jesus had been right. Now Peter was broken. His arrogance was shaken off him. This was me. I was so confident in my faith, I never believed anything could shake it, that even in his sickness I was strong. But losing Alex broke me. In my depression I was denying Jesus. I was turning away from him, pretending for everyone else my faith was just the same. This left me covered in shame. What kind of faith did I even have? Just like Peter I was humiliated, never feeling more like a failure.

5 When they entered the tomb, they saw a young man clothed in a white robe sitting on the right side. The women were shocked, 6 but the angel said, "Don't be alarmed. You are looking for Jesus of Nazareth, who was crucified. He isn't here! He is risen from the dead! Look, this is where they laid his body. 7 Now go and tell his disciples, including Peter, that Jesus is going ahead of you to Galilee. You will see him there, just as he told you before he died." Mark 16:5–7 (NLT)

Even though Peter denied Jesus, the angel specifically mentions him.

Then as the disciples are out on the water fishing Jesus appears to them from the shore. When Peter realizes it's Jesus he doesn't even wait for the boat to get to shore he jumps in and swims to Him.

15 After breakfast Jesus asked Simon Peter, "Simon son of John, do you love me more than these?"
"Yes, Lord," Peter replied, "you know I love you."
"Then feed my lambs," Jesus told him.
16 Jesus repeated the question: "Simon son of John, do you love me?" "Yes, Lord," Peter said, "you know I love you."
"Then take care of my sheep," Jesus said.
17 A third time he asked him, "Simon son of John, do you love me?" Peter was hurt that Jesus asked the question a third time. He said, "Lord, you know everything. You know that I love you." Jesus said, "Then feed my sheep.
John 21:15–17 (NLT)

Peter experiences grace. There is grace despite our denial of Jesus. There is grace despite our pride and arrogance. Just like in Peter, Jesus will allow our faith to be sifted so that God can USE the valuable part that is left. Like Peter, God knew my faith would fail. He knew I needed to be sifted in order to be used.

In 2 Corinthians 12:9 Peter says this:

Each time he said, "My grace is all you need. My power works best in weakness." So now I am glad to boast about my weaknesses, so that the power of Christ can work through me.

God is going to use my pain as a platform. It is by God's grace my faith was restored to something new. Now I no longer believe my good works are what bring God's blessings. Now I no longer believe that I will have a life without trials. Instead, I believe is God's grace through the life, death, and resurrection of Jesus *so that* I may have eternal life. This life here is not forever and I will see my son again.

A Letter from Peter 1 Peter 1:3–9

3 All praise to God, the Father of our Lord Jesus Christ. It is by his great mercy that we have been born again, because God raised Jesus Christ from the dead. Now we live with great expectation, 4 and we have a priceless inheritance—an inheritance that is kept in heaven for you, pure and undefiled, beyond the reach of change and decay. 5 And through your faith, God is protecting you by his power until you receive this salvation, which is ready to be revealed on the last day for all to see. 6 So be truly glad. There is wonderful joy ahead, even though you must endure many trials for a little while. 7 These trials will show that your faith is genuine. It is being tested as fire tests

and purifies gold—though your faith is far more precious than mere gold. So when your faith remains strong through many trials, it will bring you much praise and glory and honor on the day when Jesus Christ is revealed to the whole world.
8 You love him even though you have never seen him. Though you do not see him now, you trust him; and you rejoice with a glorious, inexpressible joy. 9 The reward for trusting him will be the salvation of your souls. (NLT)

> Has your life been vigorously shaken to sift
> the valuable from the worthless? What pain is
> God going to use for your platform?

Good Good Father
Chris Tomlin[1]
*I've heard a thousand stories of what they think
you're like But I've heard the tender whispers
of love in the dead of night And you tell me
that you're pleased And that I'm never alone*

CHAPTER EIGHT

THE PROMISE
(GOD CAN'T USE ME)

A s I have said over and over again, I am a planner therefore when our third child, our daughter was born via another c-section my doctor said we should consider surgical measures to prevent any more pregnancies. My husband was set with our two healthy kids. Although I always wanted another I could never decipher if this was a desire that stemmed from always feeling one child was missing because of Alex.

The doctors had concerns because of the amount of scar tissue from my previous C-sections and believed having a fourth C-section would be medically unsafe. All this left the ultimate decision of being done building our family as a "no brainer." Besides pregnancy is hard. Don't get me wrong, I love being pregnant. However the worrying, the high-risk status, and the countless tests I can do without.

Two years later my husband took the recommendation of my doctor and got his vasectomy. He will tell you it was pain free and heck, he got treated like a king for the weekend with meals in bed, TV, and a relatively "kid free" pass. My son, then four, was curious as to why Daddy couldn't get out of bed to play with him. My husband told him that Daddy had an owie and showed him the general area. That was that. Some sort of "man code" I presumed, or so I thought. Later that day, I overheard a neighbor say, "Oh poor Daddy." Oh crap. What is he saying to her??? I quickly asked and she replied with a chuckle he said daddy has an owie on his pee pee. Needless to say, the entire neighborhood found out Brandon had a vasectomy that weekend. I guess it's better than assuming what the "owie on his pee pee" could be!

Fast forward another two years. My son is six and my daughter is four. We are enjoying life without diapers, bottles, a diaper bag, all the large baby toys and we have regained our living room for the most part and we can walk around without stepping on or over a kazillion toys. Each time a friend has a baby my husband's favorite line is, "good for you guys," as we look at each other and chuckle … SUCKERS! With the kids getting older we finally decided to get away for the night. Since the closest grandparent is eight hours away, getting an entire night away is few and far between, but we succeeded. We lined up our best babysitter and headed out to the city for a glorious mini weekend away. While being away we even joke around about how I was ovulating but thank goodness we didn't have to worry about that! Phew!

Our church, Elevation Church, celebrated their seven-year anniversary that year and Pastor was talking about seven being "completion." Brandon and I felt really good about this. You see Elevation opened on February 5, 2006 the day we had Alex baptized at Duke Medical Center. Because of this, the church's anniversary has always been a difficult time of year for us. A time of year when the memories flood back and we jump on an emotional roller coaster. Not this year. This year we had felt good about where we were emotionally. Alex was and always will be a part of our family, but it isn't overwhelmingly sad anymore. We could look back on his life with joy and thankfulness that we were even chosen to be his parents. The biggest hurdle, our marriage, had made it! We were happy.

Well this is where things start getting really interesting because while on vacation back home to Michigan, I started to get a belly bulge, what appeared to be morning sickness, and extreme exhaustion. My husband swore it had to be something else like early menopause, fluctuating hormones, or maybe I was baking too much because I recently started my own little at-home baking business. I started to wonder "*when was my last period*?"

The worry didn't really set in until my husband and I were at lunch, waiting for his dad to meet us when he looked across the table with affection in his eyes and said, "You look so beautiful today." I became horrified because he always thinks I look the most beautiful when I am pregnant.

I immediately responded, "Take that back!! Am I glowing??" Later that day, I watched numbly as the pregnancy test lines appeared to announce I was pregnant. My mother and sister-in-law were on the other side of the bathroom door as I started screaming and crying. They began banging on the door, "What did it say?!?"

You see in my family getting a vasectomy is a right of passage when you decide your family is complete. My family began placing "Prego" jars of pasta sauce near me and everyone was joking around about Brandon's Super Sperm. All the while the women, my sister and sister-in-law, were all panicking and telling their husbands to keep their distance until they got theirs checked. Probably the best joke of the week was when my dad looked over at my mom and said, "Well Kath you think I should go get checked?" My mom just laughed and said, "No, I think we are alright!"

The next week, at eleven weeks I found myself at the doctor's office with confirmation we were indeed *pregnant*! This was definitely one of the most surprising miracles. The vasectomy has a .02% failure rate, the most effective form of birth control and yet we have somehow beat the odds. This only makes me want to fill out Publishers Clearing House that much more quickly when it arrives in the mail, because surely with these odds we are bound to win! My husband used to say in reference to his vasectomy, "they took a little piece of me that day." Now we joke that they clearly didn't take enough.

I honestly think my husband took the news much better than myself. He was blessed with a new job that would cover the costs of having a new baby in the house so I believe that was his biggest concern and it had been taken care of. For me however, I had told myself for the past four years there would be no more babies. My kids had started going off to school and with my youngest less than two years from Kindergarten I had begun dreaming of my life outside of this house even ... gasp ... the possibilities of a career again. Now my world had been turned upside down with the realization that what I had begun to dream will be placed on the back burner for another six years and who knows what I will want to do then when I am reaching forty and have been home for over ten years.

The next February came, another church anniversary, and Pastor was speaking of how the number eight means "new beginnings." Our last (fingers crossed) son was born on March 16, just three days before the eight-year anniversary of Alexander's angel day. My husband said, "He is our new beginning, a gift for our faithfulness to Him as we have continued to praise Him despite our Alex's suffering and passing." So we named this blessing Lukas Alexander.

*1 One day as Jesus was preaching on the shore of
the Sea of Galilee, great crowds pressed in on
him to listen to the word of God. 2 He noticed
two empty boats at the water's edge, for the
fishermen had left them and were washing their
nets. 3 Stepping into one of the boats, Jesus
asked Simon, its owner, to push it out into the water.
So he sat in the boat and taught the crowds from there.
Luke 5:1–3*

It may seem like something small, but Jesus wanted to use Peter's boat to teach to the crowds. Now I am realizing that Jesus wants to use me. I am a vessel, just like the boat.

> **My question for you is, "Right now, how does
> God want to use you? What boat do you have?
> You too are a vessel.**

*4 When he had finished speaking, he said to Simon, "Now go
out where it is deeper, and let down your nets to catch some
fish." 5 "Master," Simon replied, "we worked hard all last
night and didn't catch a thing. But if you say so, I'll let the nets
down again." 6 And this time their nets were so full of fish they
began to tear! 7 A shout for help brought their partners in the
other boat, and soon both boats were filled with fish and on the
verge of sinking. 8 When Simon Peter realized what had happened, he fell to his knees before Jesus and said, "Oh, Lord,
please leave me—I'm too much of a sinner to be around you."
9 For he was awestruck by the number of fish they had caught,
as were the others with him. 10 His partners, James and John,
the sons of Zebedee, were also amazed. Jesus replied to Simon,*

"Don't be afraid! From now on you'll be fishing for people!"
11 And as soon as they landed, they left everything and followed
Jesus. Luke 5:4-11

If I were Peter, I am not so sure I would've responded in the same way he did. It is possible I would allow him to use my boat. However, what happens next blows me away. Peter is a fisherman by trade. He is also the son of Jonah, a man who was swallowed by a fish for three days. Peter had been out all night fishing. Despite their giant nets and their skill, they had not caught a single fish. They were tired, frustrated, and surely ready to go home. As you can see in verse 1, they were already cleaning their nets. When I have already cleaned something the last thing I want to do, is get it dirty right away. I have even been known to eat meals outside the day I mop (weather pending), only so I can enjoy clean floors a little longer. I can say with confidence the nets would be the thing I would really not want to clean again.

This wasn't Peters response. Instead he said, "But if you say so." It was Peter's response and his actions next that allowed Jesus to bless him. If he had responded any other way, he wouldn't have been blessed the same.

For we are God's handiwork, created in Christ Jesus to do
good works, which God prepared in advance for us to do.
Ephesians 2:10

Every part of this was planned and prepared for in advance. Not my plans but His plans.

The unplanned pregnancy so early into our marriage.

Getting ICU coverage insurance.

Walking through a cemetery and wrapping my mind around

having to bury a child.

The overwhelming need to pray in the car.

Not finding Alex's heart condition before birth so Edd Shope had to airlift him to Duke—creating a lasting friendship through the loss of our sons.

The mother whose daughter passed away before Alex, providing me with an example of her courage and selflessness.

The hallway whisper where I felt God's presence surround me in the answer of "No."

Every person with whom our lives have been intertwined along the way.

Just before Alex's surgery we were approached about donating Alex's thymus gland. The thymus gland has to be removed in order to access the heart, and this doctor was doing an experimental study at Duke Medical Center to then use it for children born without a thymus, DiGeorge's anomaly. If someone is born without a thymus, there is essentially no immune system. The thymus develops the T cells (white blood cells) needed to fight off infection. There was a child in need of a thymus gland at Duke. We obliged and underwent the testing necessary to determine whether Alex's thymus could be used to correct DiGeorge's anomaly. At the time, Duke was the only Medical Center that performed this procedure. In the summer of 2007, we received a letter from Dr. Market telling us the child who received Alex's thymus tissue was alive and well because of Alex.

Several years after losing Alex, I was going through all of the things I had kept when I found the letter Dr. Lodge had mailed us, written just a few days after his death:

March 21, 2006

Mr. and Mrs. DeLeeuw:

I wanted you to know what a pleasure it was to get to know you during your son's hospitalization. Rarely have I met parents as dedicated and caring as you are. I know that Alex's illness was a surprise to you and that the entire situation was overwhelming. The understanding, compassion, humor, and strength that you faced it with were inspiring. I'm sure that you know that our team did everything we could for him while he was here. Unfortunately, things did not turn out the way any of us would have wanted. I wish that there was more that we could have done. The fact that you were able to see the positive things in his short life even at the time of his death is a lesson to us all.

I hope that as you grieve that you will turn to each other for comfort. Often times these tragic events can place great strains on relationships. I'm sure that you will be wonderful parents. If there is ever anything that I can do for you, please feel free to call me.

Yours with admiration,

Andrew J. Lodge, M.D.

These letters are on the wall in our dining room. They are a reminder that Alex's life didn't just touch us, it touched others. God orchestrated all of this. I may not understand it all right now, but I do know it continues to bring transformation to my faith.

Writing this book was something I felt called to do over ten years ago, but as you now know, I am a planner. Sharing my personal feelings and being vulnerable to others was not in my plans, so you can just call me "Jonah." In fact, years ago my friend asked me to share a series on her blog and I did. I was able to scratch the surface but didn't go too deep. I basically said to God, "OK. I wrote." The calling didn't go away. Every sermon and every book I read was a reminder. This continued until a few years ago, and then silence. He was no longer asking me to write and I couldn't have been happier. I believed He finally *heard* me. He finally *got* me.

But then (the dreaded words) we picked the work PROMISE as our word of the year. We have specific promises for our extended family that we want to see this year, none of them were for us specifically. God has other plans. He began to use my sister and friend to ask me about *that* book I was going to write. He used a women's book study group I was leading to speak to me and a sermon series "Maybe: God." The pastor even said, "Sometimes you will hear God calling you in to something, but you don't go. Don't worry, God has call waiting and He will call you back!"[1] I almost fell out of the chair. I wanted every single part of the plan laid out for me. Have I *not yet learned through all of this that God is only going to show me what I need to know, and I need to have faith in the rest?*

This journey has opened wounds, causing a paralyzing pain. It has pulled out bitterness I had pushed so deep into my soul that until I began to write in a way that was vulnerable, I was unable to recognize it. I have had to relive memories I honestly never wanted to think about again. I have had days where I am completely spent, emotionally exhausted. In all of this, not only have I found a peace in seeing just how God was with me every step of the way, but a new perspective on the support of my husband.

In the first chapter, I discussed how I had prayed the Prayer of Jabez from 1 Chronicles for three years, hoping that He would enlarge my territory. What I didn't know then, was the lineage spelled out in 1 Chronicles 4 is of Judah, which means "praise." In verse 9 the list of descendants stops with Jabez, which explains his name: "sorrow." Vance K Jackson describes it like this, "His mom called him sorrow but God called him blessed."[2] This perfectly depicts the cycle of hope: praise to sorrow to blessed. I was living a life full of praise. Even in the birth of my imperfect son, I could praise God. Then the pain brought me sorrow and anguish. Just as Jabez, despite the circumstances that surrounded me I would not stay in the sorrow, and instead choose to seek God to bless me.

In 2007, I had a student named Taylor in my Civics and Economics class. I didn't even know the impact of Alex's life on hers until years later. She posted this on her Facebook account: "I remember sitting in that desk on the left-hand side of the classroom in awe from Alex's pictures, knowing I was meant to help fighters like him." She believes it is Alex who helped her through nursing school.

In the fall of 2018, a friend of mine told me about a woman who had lost her twin girls. I reached out immediately. Through our meetings we have formed a fast friendship that has a language only "angel mommas" can understand.

God has and is using this to enlarge my territory for Him and bring hope to others. The people He brought into our lives while Alex was sick, the years following, and even now.

When I Get Where I'm Going
Brad Paisley[3]

Yeah, when I get where I'm going
There'll be only happy tears
I will shed the sins and struggles
I have carried all these years
And I'll leave my heart wide open
I will love and have no fear
Yeah, when I get where I'm going
Don't cry for me down here

CHAPTER NINE

FEAR OR FAITH
(GOD WILL ONLY USE ME
WHEN I CHOOSE FAITH)

"Two buttons in life called Love and Fear."
—*Kanye West*[1]

I love this concept of two roads; a choice. However, the roads are less about love and fear (sorry Kanye) but more about faith or fear. Maybe you are at the point where you know if given the choice of fear or faith, you would choose fear. Or maybe you can look back on your life and you have chosen fear frequently.

I want to tell you, "ME TOO!" There are often times when I look back on my life and can specifically remember when God was calling me to walk out of the boat in faith. I remember these moments so vividly because I didn't follow through. I wasn't willing to just trust God. Remember, I am a planner. I can't wrap my mind around doing something that is out of my comfort zone. I can't let go of the control I feel I need to have. The result is me saying, "What if..."

I mentioned before that throughout college I was trained to be a YL leader. I led YL during my college years, raised up and trained other leaders, attended additional training through what they call *Student Staff.* I spent summers working at camps. I was on the track to be on the YL staff. I even asked my parents to attend YL camp my final summer of leading in my college town so they would "buy" into it. It worked. They loved it. However, I was still sitting on the boat. I couldn't bear to step out in faith and walk on water toward the path where I knew God was leading me. It wasn't because I didn't love YL, I did. It wasn't because I didn't trust God, I did. It was because it was not what I had planned for my life. I went to school to be a teacher. I didn't go to school to then have to raise my own income each year. That seemed too risky. Besides, wouldn't I disappoint my parents who had paid for my college education? Instead, I turned my head and watched other people do it.

After studying when Peter was walking on water, I thought about those still left on the boat. Why didn't anyone else step out? Was their faith not as strong?

22 Immediately Jesus made the disciples get into the boat and go on ahead of him to the other side, while he dismissed the crowd. 23 After he had dismissed them, he went up on a mountainside by himself to pray. Later that night, he was there alone, 24 and the boat was already a considerable distance from land, buffeted by the waves because the wind was against it. 25 Shortly before dawn Jesus went out to them, walking on the lake. 26 When the disciples saw him walking on the lake, they were terrified. "It's a ghost," t hey said, and cried out in fear. 27 But Jesus immediately said to them: "Take courage! It is I. Don't be afraid." 28 "Lord, if it's you," Peter replied,

"tell me to come to you on the water." 29 "Come,"
he said. Then Peter got down out of the boat,
walked on the water and came toward Jesus.
Matthew 14:22–33

Perhaps the disciples were so crippled with fear they weren't able to move and could only observe. I have been there too. When I watched a friend accomplish the dream that had been in my heart, it crippled me. I wasn't empowered to say, "If she can do it, so can I!" Instead, it made me more fearful, and I began to question myself. *Why did this dream come to fruition for her and not me? What am I doing wrong? Why doesn't God want to use me?* Even to the point of outright jealousy, "How dare she take *my* dream!" Gulp.

For the disciples, the sea was deeper than they could measure despite the many times it was attempted. There was a legitimate fear that under the sea was the underworld.[2] Therefore, when the disciples saw Jesus they believed him to be a ghost that rose up in the storm. Maybe you have a specific storm in your life right now where you have a very real legitimate fear: losing a house, kids, spouse, or even your own health. Like the disciples, the idea of a ghost outweighs the hope of Jesus.

30 But when he saw the wind, he was afraid and,
beginning to sink, cried out, "Lord, save me!"

Perhaps it was because the elements still weren't fit for trusting Jesus. Did that pinch a nerve for you? Yep. I have been there too. We think, even to the point of "negotiate," if God will just do A, B, and C, then I will do what He is asking. If you will calm these waves (debt, job loss, cancer, etc.) I am drowning in first, then I will trust you. Or if you can calm down the winds (crumbling marriage, disobedient kids, career that is going nowhere, loneliness, etc.) that keep knocking me over, then I will do what you are calling me to.

31 Immediately Jesus reached out his hand and caught him. "You of little faith," he said, "why did you doubt?"

Perhaps Jesus said it loudly enough for the other disciples to hear? Is it possible this is a reminder not only to the one who took the risk to step out in faith and lost his focus, but also to the ones who remained on the boat?

32 And when they climbed into the boat, the wind died down. 33 Then those who were in the boat worshiped him, saying, "Truly you are the Son of God.

Perhaps the disciples just weren't ready to trust. Perhaps they didn't see it until this very moment. I often find myself in this situation, too. I have seen God's inner workings in my life and yet I still struggle to believe if it is really for my own good. I can imagine that after this, some of the disciples may have felt angry or annoyed they didn't realize it sooner.

Perhaps the disciples were even jealous that Peter stepped off the boat. Recently I was pushed down by my jealousy. It came on so quickly I didn't even expect it. I was jealous of another family whose child has HLHS and is living. I was jealous because, as they spoke about their "miracle," "blessing," and "answered prayers," I was crying out *"What about me?!"* I was angry because I *had* stepped out of the boat in faith during this time and yet my prayer was not answered in a miracle. My prayer was answered, but not in the way I wanted.

Even with all the mentions of "perhaps," there is a lesson in the boat. If you choose to be Peter and step out in faith, God will bless you. You may lose sight of Jesus and begin to drown, but God is always there to grab the hand that is reaching for him to pull you up. This decision of faith over fear is constant. It is not a one-and-done choice. You will be faced with this repeatedly.

When we choose fear over faith, and we all do, there is still hope for us! The other disciples who faced the storm saw what they believed to be a ghost walking on water, watched Peter step out in faith, and heard Jesus rebuke their little faith, were still used. They didn't get to shore and Jesus said, "Well guys, I am only going to take Peter the rest of the way." No, the disciples remained with Jesus. They witnessed His miracles and were then used to expand the Kingdom.

It is encouraging to me to know that even when I choose fear, God doesn't turn from me. Even when I decide it is too hard, painful, or not well enough planned for my liking, God waits for me. I absolutely miss out on what He has ready for me in the moment. I absolutely will not be used in the exact same way as if I step out of the boat. But just like the other disciples, I can still be used for great things!

I don't know your journey, but I do know that every single one of us experiences loss: of a job, of a child/spouse/parents/ sibling, of a friendship that slips away, or of a failed dream. We have all had a different "plan" than what came forth.

Right now, are you standing in a current of fear, in faith, or in pain that is making it hard to even take a breath? My hope is in your pain you can see purpose. I hope that even if you are still in the midst of your pain you can begin to have a "hallway whisper"; those moments when you know God is whispering to you that you will be okay. You are not alone. Keep your eyes above the waves, find the lighthouse pattern, and reach out your hand to be pulled up. Hope is on the horizon.

Oceans (Where Feet May Fail)
Hillsong UNITED[3]

Your grace abounds in deepest waters
Your sovereign hand
Will be my guide
Where feet may fail and fear surrounds me
You've never failed and You won't start now

FEAR OR FAITH

ACKNOWLEDGEMENTS

Brandon, you have pushed me when I didn't want to be pushed to finish. You have been my rock and will always be my "hot summer fling." There is no one else I'd rather have in my corner. It is an honor to be in this journey with you.

Xavier, Irelyn, and Lukas, you are all my rainbows after the storm. Xavier when you read the first chapter and told me it was the best thing you have ever read encouraged me more than you will ever know. You guys are the reason I can get up each day and smile. Ten second hug!

Angie and Erica, you both were a driving force to get me writing again. Over the course of this journey you have checked on me and kept me in check. Thanks for not letting me quit.

Amy, I can't imagine anyone else designing the cover. You know this story from the inside out and have been my co-pilot for over 20 years.

Jessica, you have been my sounding board throughout this whole process. Always willing to read everything I send your way. I am so grateful for your friendship.

Dr. Andrew Lodge, no words can express how grateful we are for your continuous care for our family. You gave us extra time with our son and are continuing to help us build a legacy. Thank you for writing the foreword for this book and for encouraging me to press forward in this venture.

Dr. Cindy Barrett, Jenny, Amy, Alicia, Colleen, Kristy, Denise, Jack, Brian, and so many others who loved on our Little Man while at Duke Medical Center, we are forever grateful for your care.

Edd and Tamma Shope, thank you for allowing me to share Michael in this story. I am thankful for your friendship.

My parents, Steven and Kathryn Main, you have always been my biggest cheerleader. From every dance class, competitions, and games to every phone call where I "need you" in parenthood you have been there to encourage, pick me up, and wipe away the tears. There are not enough pages to express my gratitude for your love and support.

Our family, friends, church family, and so many people who have come in our lives along the way, thank you for being a part of this journey.

ACKNOWLEDGEMENTS

NOTES

Chapter One:

1. Bruce Wilkinson and David Kopp, The Prayer of Jabez: Breaking through to the Blessed Life. (Thorndike Press, 2004).

2. Jimmie Davis Lyrics - You Are My Sunshine, Accessed July 12, 2019, https://www.lyricfinder.org/lyrics/2091126-jimmie-davis?track=you-are-my-sunshine.

Chapter Two:

1. Oprah, "Devon Franklin: Produced by Faith – Oprah's SuperSoul Conversations – Podcast," Podtail, January 30, 2019, https://podtail.com/en/podcast/oprah-s-supersoul-conversations/devon-franklin-pro-duced-by-faith/.

2. "Congenital Heart Defects - Facts about Hypoplastic Left Heart Syndrome | CDC." Centers for Disease Control and Prevention. Accessed July 12, 2019. https://www.cdc.gov/ncbddd/heartdefects/hlhs.html.

3. "Home - PubMed - NCBI." National Center for Biotechnology Information. Accessed May 24, 2011. https://www.ncbi.nlm.nih.gov/pubmed.

4. "Oswald Chambers Quotes (Author of My Utmost for His Highest)." Goodreads. Accessed July 12, 2019. https://www.goodreads.com/author/quotes/41469.Oswald_Chambers.

5. Todd Burpo. Heaven Is For Real (Thomas Nelson, 2010), 42.

6. Max Lucado. Fearless (Thomas Nelson, 2009).

7. Lauren Daigle Lyrics - You Say. Accessed July 12, 2019, https://www.lyricfinder.org/lyrics/35327262-lauren-daigle?track=you-say.

Chapter Three:

1. Steven Furtick. Sun Stand Still: What Happens When You Dare to Ask God for the Impossible (Multnomah Books, 2010), 65.

2. "It Is So." Elevation Worship. Accessed January 30, 2020. https://elevationworship.com/song-resources/it-is-so/.

Chapter Four:

1. Debbie Macomber, One Simple Act: Discovering the Power of Generosity (New York: Howard Books, 2019), 156.

2. "Better Is One Day Lyrics and Chords: Worship Together." Better Is One Day Lyrics and Chords | Worship Together. Accessed July 12, 2019. https://www.worshiptogether.com/songs/better-is-one-day/.

3. William P. Young, The Shack: A Novel by (Los Angeles: Windblown Media, 2007), 230.

4. Jack Johnson and Matt Costa Lyrics - Lullaby. Accessed July 12, 2019. https://www.lyricfinder.org/lyrics/8620808-jack-johnson-and-matt-costa-lullaby.

5. Max Lucado, Fearless (Thomas Nelson, 2009), 64.

Chapter Five:

1. "The Weepies – World Spins Madly On." Genius, January 1, 2006. https://genius.com/The-weepies-world-spins-madly-on-lyrics.

Chapter Six:

1. "A History of Lighthouses." Project Archaeology. October 31, 2018. Accessed March 13, 2019. https://projectarchaeology.org/2016/08/01/a-history-of-lighthouses/.

2. Max Lucado, Outlive Your Life (Thomas Nelson Publishers, 2010), 159.

3. "Beyond Boston Light: 300 Years of America's First Lighthouse." Time. Accessed March 13, 2019. https://time.com/4489223/lighthouse-american-history/.

4. Rend Collective Lyrics - My Lighthouse. Accessed July 12, 2019. https://www.lyricfinder.org/lyrics/31145378-rend-collective?track=my-lighthouse.

Chapter Seven:

1. Chris Tomlin Lyrics - Good Good Father. Accessed July 13, 2019. https://www.lyricfinder.org/lyrics/32245645-chris-tomlin?track=-good-good-father.

Chapter Eight:

1. Furtick, Steven, "Maybe: God- I'm Confused About My Calling" (Elevation Church, February 10, 2019).

2. Jackson, Vance K. "1." Enlarge - Vance K. Jackson Leads Readers through One of the Bible's Most Powerful, Destiny Shifting Prayers Declared by a Man Named - Jabez. "Enlarge" Was Designed to Unleash Your Prayer Life and to Stretch You beyond the Boundaries of Normalcy. Through You, God Wants to Break Generational Cycles and Transform Your Family - Forever. Accessed May 26, 2019. https://www.bible.com/reading-plans/14173-enlarge/day/2.

3. Dolly Parton and Brad Paisley Lyrics - When I Get Where I'm Going. Accessed July 13, 2019. https://www.lyricfinder.org/lyrics/8274770-dolly-parton-and-brad-paisley?track=when-i-get-where-im-going.

Chapter Nine:

1. "My Next Guest Needs No Introduction With David Letterman/Kanye West." In My Next Guest Needs No Introduction With David Letterman. Netflix. 2019.

2. Adam Hamilton. Simon Peter: Flawed but Faithful Disciple (Nashville,

TN: Abingdon Press, 2018), 47.

3. Hillsong United Lyrics - Oceans (Where Feet May Fail). Accessed July 13, 2019. https://www.lyricfinder.org/lyrics/28962078-hillsong-united?track=oceans-where-feet-may-fail.

NOTES

ABOUT THE AUTHOR

C andice and her husband, Brandon, have been married for well over a decade and experienced more in their first year of marriage then most marriages ever will. They have four children and are what keeps them motivated, laughing, and working (they are expensive!).

Candice is powered through her faith in Jesus Christ and her passion to share on the hope only He can provide after loss. Congenital Heart Defects occur in 1 of every 100 births making it the most common birth defect. Their first-born son, Alexander, was born with Hypo-plastic Left Heart Syndrome. When he was six days old he underwent open heart surgery. He fought for 52 days.

Candice's newest adventures include founding Hope in Healing Hearts LLC, speaking on The Hope Journey and Season Support (how to support others through difficult seasons), and writing weekly blogs on candicedeleeuw.com. Candice believes in the importance of helping other mom's through their journey and empowering them to find purpose in their pain.

When not writing, Candice is teaching for Stanly Community College and leading a women's eGroup for Elevation Church.

Most days you can find her in the Charlotte area on the sideline of a soccer game, at the dance studio, or reading a book, but always with a coffee in hand.

Candice would love to connect with you. Reach out at:

candice@candicedeleeuw.com
https://www.facebook.com/candicedeleeuw.author/
https://www.instagram.com/candice_deleeuw/

ABOUT THE AUTHOR

Hope in Healing Hearts

HOPE IN HEALING HEARTS

In 2006, our world was turned upside down when we heard the devastating news our son, Alexander, was born with a congenital heart defect, Hypoplastic Left Heart Syndrome. Alex underwent open heart surgery when he was six days old and fought for seven weeks. When we had to walk away from the hospital for the final time our world stopped spinning. We had no one to turn to and no resources to get us through. We felt incredibly alone and was unsure what was "normal" in our grief. For months I read countless books on grief and child loss. However, I could never find the book that met my desire to find hope and healing.

As I began to write the book I couldn't find, it became clear I needed to give this book to other parents who find themselves in this new upside down world just like we did. In doing so, we have founded HHH LLC, a for good company. For every book sold, we are giving all the profit to give this book away to parents after child loss.

At HHH, our mission is to provide hope through resources and community for those who are healing from life's heartbreaks.

Our vision is so that parents do not feel alone in their journey after child loss, while battling childhood anxiety, climbing the highs and lows of marriage, or any life event that causes heartbreak.

If you are a parent who received this book because of the generosity of others and would like to share your story please email Candice at candice@candicedeleeuw.com

Interested in partnering with us?
Check out the opportunities at:

hopeinhealinghearts.org.

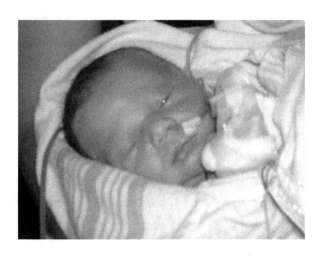